MW00762412

Need to Know Basics—
College

Christopher D. Hudson

Maryann Lackland

Amber Rae

Randy Southern

Linda Taylor

Linda Washington

Len Woods

BARBOUR
PUBLISHING

Need to Know Basics—College
Copyright © 2003 by Barbour Publishing, Inc.
All rights reserved.

ISBN 1-58660-988-2

Check out Barbour's exciting web site at: www.barbourbooks.com

Unless otherwise noted, Scripture is taken from THE HOLY BIBLE, NEW INTERNATIONAL VERSION, Copyright © 1973, 1979, 1984, by International Bible Society. Used by permission of Zondervan Publishing House.

Scripture quotations marked KJV are taken from The Holy Bible, King James Version.

Scripture quotations marked NKJV are taken from The Holy Bible, New King James Version. Copyright © 1979, 1980, 1982 by Thomas Nelson, Inc. Used by permission. All rights reserved.

Scripture quotations marked NLT are taken from The Holy Bible, New Living Translation, copyright © 1996. Used by permission of Tyndale House Publishers, Inc., Wheaton, Illinois 60189, U.S.A. All rights reserved.

Produced with the assistance of the Livingstone Corporation (www.Livingstonecorp.com). Project staff includes Christopher D. Hudson, Ashley Taylor, Rosalie Krusemark, and Greg Longbons.

Interior Design by Design Corps, Batavia, IL.

Cover Design by Robyn Martins.

Cover and Interior Artwork by Elwood Smith.

Published by: Barbour Publishing, Inc., P.O. Box 719, Uhrichsville, OH 44683

Member of the
Evangelical Christian
Publishers Association

Printed in the United States of America.
5 4 3 2 1

Table of Contents

Section 7
Being a Christian College Student 116

Section 8
Friendships and Dating 133

Section 9
Campus Life 149

Section 10
Leaving School 169

Introduction

You've heard it said that the "college years are the best years of your life." While the college years are exciting, that statement is not entirely true. Most people find excitement in many areas of life: high school, marriage, parenting, even in the thrill of a new job.

But college is a unique four- or five-year experience. It's probably the only time in your life you'll have such a diverse group of friends, live in a dorm, and stay up all hours of the night. College is a time to discover yourself, learn how God made you, and choose a direction for your life.

That puts a lot of pressure on you to pick a good school. After you find it, you need to:

    1) figure out how to pay for it
    2) enjoy yourself and
    3) learn a few things while you're there.

Relax. It's not as hard as you think. This book will help you get there. Between these covers you'll find valuable information to help you decide where you should go to school and what you should do once you get there. Inside you'll find:

CATCH A CLUE

A Truckload of Clues. You'll learn tips from people who have successfully made it through college. They've learned a lot about getting the most out of college. While they've learned some of it the hard way, it's all here so you don't have to.

WIDE ANGLE

Perspective. Sometimes we get caught up in details of college life. To make the best decision, though, we need help looking at the whole picture. We'll help you take a step back.

WOW!

Humorous Stories and Incredible Facts. Many people associate college with having a good time. While there's certainly more to it than that, we've collected some of the best college stories for you to enjoy.

DON'T FORGET

Important Reminders. Certain things are important to remember if you ever plan on graduating (which, by the way, we highly recommend). We've highlighted those for you.

THE BOTTOM LINE

The Bottom Line. We'll help you get beyond confusion by letting you know the most important stuff to remember.

THE BIBLE SAYS

Help from Above. We've highlighted a few key Bible verses that will encourage you and help you as you plan for, then make it through college.

College is an exciting time. Before you check out one more school or make any more plans, there's one critical thing you need to do: *read this book*. Feel free to read it *your* way: from cover to cover or skipping around to the parts that interest you most. No matter how you read it, you'll find it's jammed with good advice, great ideas, and funny stories. So turn the page and start reading. . . . You'll be glad you did!

Section I
Getting Ready

What Schools Are Out There?

THE END IS NEAR

You can almost smell the ink on your last high school yearbook. Now it's time to think about college. But what college? Choosing a college is one of the most important decisions you'll make. After all, this will be your home for the next four or more years. But choosing a college doesn't have to *seem* like rocket science. Remember, God does promise to give you wisdom when you need it: "If any of you lacks wisdom, he should ask God, who gives generously to all without finding fault, and it will be given to him" (James 1:5).

There are steps you can take to make your search more informed. First, decide whether you'd like to commute or go away to school. Second, decide what type of school you'd like to attend. Consider the options.

CATCH A CLUE

Choosing a School

A woman in my church who had gone to Westmont College (in Santa Barbara, California) took me out to lunch and told me about how great it was. She was intentional about wanting me to go. She told me how neat it was and how pretty it was. So that's where I went.
—Marilyn, Salt Lake City, UT

IVY LEAGUE SCHOOLS

Wondering which schools are Ivy League? There are eight.

- Brown University (Providence, Rhode Island)
- Columbia College (New York City—part of Columbia University)
- Cornell University (Ithaca, New York)
- Dartmouth College (Hanover, Hew Hampshire)
- Harvard University [Harvard and Radcliffe Colleges] (Cambridge, Massachusetts—still the nation's top university)
- Princeton University (Princeton, New Jersey)

- University of Pennsylvania (Philadelphia, Pennsylvania)
- Yale University (New Haven, Connecticut)

Ivy League schools are among the top universities in the country. Some of them have been around for over 250 years (or over 300 in Harvard's case). Your high school GPA and SAT/ACT scores will have a direct effect on whether you make it into an Ivy League school or not. But even a perfect 800 SAT score won't guarantee admission. Since many students apply, these schools also look for the well-rounded student. How involved are you in community affairs? What is your class rank? In what extracurricular activities are you involved? Admissions officials want to know.

ALMOST "IVIES"

Some schools are just as competitive as the Ivy League schools. You'll find the following on any list of the top schools in the country. (See also the list of the top 25 national universities.)

- California Institute of Technology (Pasadena, California)
- Duke University (Durham, North Carolina)
- Johns Hopkins University (Baltimore, Maryland)
- Massachusetts Institute of Technology (Cambridge, Massachusetts)
- Northwestern University (Evanston, Illinois)
- Stanford University (Stanford, California)
- Swarthmore College (Swarthmore, Pennsylvania)
- Tufts University (Medford, Massachusetts)
- University of Chicago (Chicago, Illinois)
- University of Notre Dame (South Bend, Indiana)

BIG TEN CONFERENCE SCHOOLS

If you like a combination of sports and academics, consider these:

- Indiana University (Bloomington)
- Michigan State University (East Lansing)

- Northwestern University (Evanston, Illinois)
- Ohio State University (Columbus)
- Pennsylvania State University (State College)
- Purdue University (West Lafayette, Indiana)
- University of Illinois–Urbana/Champaign
- University of Iowa (Iowa City)
- University of Michigan (Ann Arbor)
- University of Minnesota–Twin Cities (Minneapolis–St. Paul)
- University of Wisconsin–Madison

STATE COLLEGES OR UNIVERSITIES

These schools receive government funding, making them more affordable, especially for in-state students. The University of Illinois–Urbana/Champaign, Ohio State University, SUNY (State University of New York) schools, and such are public.

PRIVATE COLLEGES

Wheaton College, Harvard University, and Calvin College are private schools, and they are not government subsidized. They can be more selective about the students they accept. These schools receive their moneys from alumni donations and tuition. In-state and out-of-state students are charged the same amount of tuition.

SINGLE-SEX COLLEGES

Some students opt for single-sex colleges because of a particular field of study. Some just want to get away from the distractions of the opposite sex. Barnard College (New York City), Mount Holyoke College (South Hadley, Massachusetts), Smith College (Northampton, Massachusetts), and Wellesley College (Wellesley, Massachusetts) are women's colleges with the same prestige as that of the Ivy League schools.

LIBERAL ARTS COLLEGES

You'll see this term used a lot in your college search. A liberal arts college is one with a program for a broad range of study (history, languages, literature, mathematics, the sciences, philosophy, and so on). Many liberal arts colleges are private. Swarthmore College is a private liberal arts college.

JUNIOR, COMMUNITY, AND TECHNICAL COLLEGES

These institutions offer an associate's degree in two years of study. The education received in a junior or community college is equal to the first two years of a four-year undergraduate college. The difference between a junior college and a community college is that junior colleges are usually private, while community colleges are public institutions that serve a specific community.

Technical schools, however, emphasize programs for technical fields (for example, computers). Some junior colleges are also known as technical colleges because of the courses they offer.

Many students who don't feel ready for a larger college choose a junior college

WIDE ANGLE

Questions to Think About

• Should I go away to college or commute?
• What type of school most interests me? (Ivy League? Big Ten Conference? Single-sex college? Coed college? Private college? Public?)
• How can I find out more information on the schools of my choice? (Should I get information on-line? Call each school for a catalogue? Call each school and make an appointment? Ask my guidance counselor?)

as an option. Afterward, they transfer to a college offering a bachelor's degree. Some junior colleges offer a bachelor's degree. These are called *two-year upper-division colleges.* Some technological and vocational schools offer associate's degrees after two to three years of study.

WEB SITES

If you need more help, visit the site of the college of your choice on-line. Or use these sites or search engines to find more information or even to apply to the school of your choice.

THE BIBLE SAYS

Get This First

"How much better to get wisdom than gold, to choose understanding rather than silver!" (Proverbs 16:16)

- www.collegenet.com (the gateway to the IBM global campus; good for information on four-year, community, technical, and junior colleges)

- www.collegexpress.com

- www.collegeview.com (an *excellent* resource with listings of over 3,700 colleges and universities)

- www.gospelcom.net (the gateway to hundreds of Christian organizations, resources, colleges, and so on)

- www.petersons.com

- www.familyeducation.com

- CollegeBoard Online (AOL—under Research & Learning)

- www.ed.gov/pubs/Prepare (another excellent resource with information to help your parents as they assist you in your college search)

- www.yahoo.com/Education (the gateway to hundreds of other sites, including www.collegeedge.com—touted as the number one web site with 52,000 pages of information on colleges, scholarships, and other details)

- www.aol.com

- www.yahoo.com

- www.csearch.kaplan.com

What to Look for in a College

You can choose to be wise as you choose a college. Depending on your life plans, the school you choose now will matter a great deal. It can affect the grad school you choose, if you decide to go further in your college education. It might also affect future ministry/internship/job opportunities. As you think about a possible major, your choice will also be affected. What do you need to look for when choosing a college? Here are some points to consider:

ACADEMICS PROGRAM

Choose a college that has a good academic reputation. Make sure the college is accredited by a reliable organization, for example, the Christian College Coalition. This means that the college has met the required standards for education. You'll want a school with a good library and good resources. Find out what majors have the strongest programs. Consider a college that is known for having a good program in the field of your choice. For example, if you're looking for a strong campus ministries program, Eastern College in Philadelphia is one school to consider. If the theater beckons, Northwestern University in Evanston and Carnegie Mellon University in Pittsburgh are two schools with top theater departments. Keep in mind that you're not locked into a major at this time. You might change your mind later.

The World Wide Web can help you explore your choices. Check out the web sites of several colleges. (See the list of web sites on page 6.) Then make an appointment to visit the campuses of your top four or five choices.

In what course of study are you thinking about majoring?

Schools that have a good reputation in this field:
-
-
-

DISTINGUISHED FACULTY

Good academics and good professors go hand in hand. You'll want to get the best education for your money, so consider a college with a good faculty. A school like Harvard has had several Nobel prize-winning professors.

CAMPUS SIZE AND ENROLLMENT

What part of the country would you consider ideal for college? Would you prefer to be close to home or a million light-years away? If you salivate at the sight of a lovely, tree-lined campus near the ocean or one in the mountains 1,000 miles from your parents, just remember this: looks aren't everything. You also need to consider what campus size suits you best. For example:

Large. Over 7,000 students. Ohio State University has over 50,000 students! The University of Illinois (Urbana/Champaign) has over 30,000. A large student body means a large campus or campuses. Better bring a bike!

Medium. Schools with about 3,000–7,000 students.

Small. Under 3,000 students.

If you like a cozy atmosphere, a large campus with 30,000 other students may not be right for you. Consider also the faculty-to-student ratio. Less faculty and more students can mean you'll get to know your teaching assistant rather than your professor. If large classes of 800 or more students make you feel too anonymous, think about a college that offers more personal attention.

The Advice of Alumni

CATCH A CLUE

Nothing beats firsthand knowledge. Someone who has attended a college you're considering can give you the best advice. But consider the source. If you know the person has a negative outlook (no matter how positive the circumstances), you might want to take what he or she says with a grain of salt.

Campus size that best suits you: _____

Schools that are this size:
-
-
-

FINANCIAL AID PACKAGE

As you know, college isn't free. Consider a college that is afford-able or offers you a good financial aid package or scholarship/work-study opportunities. You don't want to spend the rest of your life trying to pay back astronomical student loans.

The Campus Visit

Once you've narrowed down your college choices to four or five, think about a campus visit. Why? you might ask. A campus visit is a good way to determine if a school is right for

Do Your Homework

"Therefore be as shrewd as snakes and as innocent as doves." (Matthew 10:16)

WIDE ANGLE

you. A visit takes you beyond the edges of a snappy college brochure and into reality. You can set up an overnight visit, an interview, or a tour. But before you get carried away by the lure of a lovely setting, there are a few things you can do to make your visit an educated one. As Jesus once said during his Sermon on the Mount:

ASK AND IT WILL BE GIVEN TO YOU

During your visit, be sure that you or your parents ask plenty of questions. After all, this is your education. The person who takes you around the campus—whether an admissions staffer or a stu-dent—is there to help. Keep in mind that the only "stupid" ques-tion is the one that remains unasked.

Talking to students is the best way to get to know a school. Have them talk about what's beyond the school's brochure. Be sure to take notes.

If you're visiting a school in a different part of the country, don't forget to ask about the weather. What is it really like in the winter? spring? fall? One student on the Internet described how depressed she had been during her first winter at her chosen college. She had not known what type of weather conditions she could expect.

SEEK AND YOU WILL FIND

More than likely, you'll be shown a typical dorm room (clean of course), the administration buildings, and some of the academic halls during your visit. If you can, however, wander around the campus yourself. Then try to visit some off-campus spots. The more you see of the campus and the area surrounding it, the better you'll know whether you want to attend that school.

KNOCK AND THE DOOR WILL BE OPENED

An overnight visit is a good way to find out what life is really like. First, call the

CATCH A CLUE

Questions to Ask

What is the male/female ratio?
What are the freshmen classes like?

Can I get the dorm I want or are the dorms preselected for freshmen?

What feedback have you heard from minority students about the college?

How is the food (really)?

What do you like best about the school (or dislike)?

What are the class sizes like?

Are the professors approachable? Why or why not?

Do you find it easy or hard to get an appointment with a professor? Why?

What was your overall impression when you were a freshman on this campus?

admissions office to make a reservation for an overnight stay. While you're on campus, eat in the dorm, sit in a class, visit the admissions and financial aid offices, check out the library. Letting the school's admissions office know that you're visiting shows that you're interested.

If you can, visit a campus when classes are in session. Try to avoid a weekend like Homecoming. Exciting events do not provide an accurate impression of daily campus life. As you walk about the campus, keep asking those questions. Keep your eyes and ears open. The best impression you can get of a college is that of an eyewitness: *you*.

A Good Rep

"A good name is more desirable than great riches." (Proverbs 22:1)

THE BIBLE SAYS

Top Private Schools

If you're looking for a private school with a good reputation, take a look at this list. The schools are ranked by *U.S. News & World Report* for 2003. (For other schools see the *U.S. News & World Report* site [www.usnews.com].) Each school below is in rank order.

THE TOP TEN NATIONAL UNIVERSITIES

• Princeton University (Princeton, New Jersey)

• Harvard University (Cambridge, Massachusetts)

• Yale University (New Haven, Connecticut)

• California Institute of Technology (Pasadena)

• Duke University (Durham, North Carolina)

• Massachusetts Institute of Technology (Cambridge)

• Stanford University (Stanford, California)

• University of Pennsylvania (Philadelphia; not to be confused with Penn State)

• Dartmouth College (Hanover, New Hampshire)

• Columbia University (New York, New York)

TOP FIVE NATIONAL LIBERAL ARTS COLLEGES

- Amherst College (Amherst, Massachusetts)
- Swarthmore College (Swarthmore, Pennsylvania)
- Williams College (Williamstown, Massachusetts)
- Wellesley College (Wellesley, Massachusetts)
- Carleton College (Northfield, Minnesota)

For other colleges, check out a guide like *Newsweek and Kaplan Getting into College* or *The Fiske Guide to Colleges* by Edward B. Fiske (Sourcebooks). Be sure to look for the current year's guide. Also, visit the sites listed in "What Schools Are Out There?"

CATCH A CLUE

Stay Close to Home?

"Jesus grew in wisdom and stature, and in favor with God and men." (Luke 2:52)

Jesus grew in knowledge and favor close to home. You can too. For the best state schools, you can't beat the schools on the list below. See the *U.S. News & World Report* site for other schools (www.usnews.com). Each school is in rank order.

Top State Schools

TOP FIVE NATIONAL UNIVERSITIES

- University of California–Berkeley
- University of Virginia (Charlottesville)
- University of California–Los Angeles
- University of Michigan–Ann Arbor
- University of North Carolina–Chapel Hill

ANOTHER LIST

Money Magazine offers this list as their top ten. The list includes public and private universities. (See www.money.com for their reasons for ranking the colleges and for other college information.)

- California Institute of Technology (Pasadena)
- Rice University (Houston, Texas)
- University of North Carolina–Chapel Hill
- SUNY at Binghamton (Binghamton, New York City)
- Spelman College (Atlanta, Georgia)
- New College of the University of South Florida (Sarasota)
- College of New Jersey (Trenton)
- Truman State University (Kirksville, Missouri)
- SUNY College–Geneseo
- University of Florida–Gainesville

Top Christian Schools

If you'd like to combine ministry with study, a Christian college may be ideal for you. Although there is no official ranking of Christian colleges, the following are considered by many to be among the best in the country. Some of the following are members of the Coalition for Christian Colleges and Universities while some are Christian College Consortium schools. (Some are members of both.) You will also find some of these schools listed among the top national universities.

Christian Education

"Preach the Word; be prepared in season and out of season; correct, rebuke and encourage—with great patience and careful instruction." (2 Timothy 4:2)

THE BIBLE SAYS

- Calvin College—Grand Rapids, Michigan (ranked among the top of the Christian colleges)
- Biola University—La Mirada, California
- Eastern College—St. Davids, Pennsylvania (multiethnic student body draws minority students)
- Fresno Pacific College—Fresno, California

- North Park College—Chicago, Illinois (multiethnic student body draws minority students)
- Point Loma Nazarene College—San Diego, California

According to *The Fiske Guide to Colleges*, the following are some of the top evangelical liberal arts schools.

- Asbury College—Wilmore, Kentucky
- Bethel College—St. Paul, Minnesota
- George Fox College—Newberg, Oregon
- Gordon College—Wenham, Massachusetts (also ranked as one of the top national liberal arts colleges)
- Greenville College—Greenville, Illinois
- Houghton—Houghton, New York
- Malone College—Canton, Ohio
- Messiah College—Grantham, Pennsylvania (considered a good environment for minority students)
- Seattle Pacific University—Seattle, Washington
- Taylor University—Upland, Indiana
- Trinity College—Deerfield, Illinois
- Westmont College—Santa Barbara, California
- Wheaton College—Wheaton, Illinois (viewed as the finest evangelical college in the country)

CATCH A CLUE

Questions to Think About

Why do I want to attend a Christian school? (This is a question to think deeply about.)

Which schools have the academic programs I want?

How will this school affect or aid the ministry to which God has called me?

Can I afford this school?

Education on a Budget

Looking for a more affordable school? Then use wisdom as you consider the following lists of public and private schools, compiled by *The Fiske Guide to Colleges*. (See state-by-state list beginning on page 18 also for additional schools.) Be sure to research carefully the quality of education in each school.

PUBLIC COLLEGES AND UNIVERSITIES

- University of Alabama–Tuscaloosa
- University of Arizona (Tucson)
- University of Arkansas (Fayetteville)
- College of Charleston (South Carolina)

Make Yourself Better

"I, wisdom, dwell together with prudence; I possess knowledge and discretion." (Proverbs 8:12)

THE BIBLE SAYS

- CUNY (City University of New York)–Brooklyn College
- CUNY–City College of New York
- CUNY–Hunter College
- CUNY–Queens College
- University of Delaware (Newark)
- Evergreen State College (Olympia, Washington)
- Florida State University (Tallahassee)
- University of Florida (Gainesville)
- University of Georgia (Athens)
- University of Houston (Texas)
- University of Iowa (Iowa City)
- University of Kansas (Lawrence)
- University of Maine–Orono
- University of Minnesota–Morris
- University of Minnesota–Twin Cities (Minneapolis)

- Montana Tech of the University of Montana (Butte)
- University of Nebraska–Lincoln
- New College of the University of South Florida (Sarasota)
- University of New Mexico (Albuquerque)
- North Carolina State University (Raleigh)
- University of North Carolina–Asheville
- University of North Carolina–Chapel Hill
- University of North Carolina–Greensboro
- Ohio State University (Columbus)
- University of Oklahoma (Norman)
- University of Oregon (Eugene)
- Purdue University (West Lafayette, Indiana)
- University of South Carolina (Columbia)
- University of Tennessee–Knoxville
- Truman State University (Kirksville, Missouri)
- Virginia Polytechnic Institute and State University (Blacksburg)
- West Virginia University (Morgantown)
- College of William and Mary (Williamsburg, Virginia)

PRIVATE COLLEGES AND UNIVERSITIES

- Albertson College (Caldwell, Idaho)
- Alma College (Alma, Michigan)
- Alverno College (Milwaukee, Wisconsin)
- Austin College (Sherman, Texas)
- Baylor University (Waco, Texas)
- Birmingham–Southern College (Alabama)
- Calvin College (Grand Rapids, Michigan)
- Cooper Union (New York City)
- University of Dallas (Irving, Texas)
- University of Dayton (Dayton, Ohio)

- DePaul University (Chicago)
- Florida Institute of Technology (Melbourne, Florida)
- Gordon College (Wenham, Massachusetts)
- Guilford College (Greensboro, North Carolina)
- Gustavus Adolphus College (St. Peter, Minnesota)
- Hendrix College (Conway, Arkansas)
- Hofstra University (Hempstead, New York)
- Hope College (Holland, Michigan)
- Houghton College (Houghton, New York)
- Howard University (Washington, D.C.)
- Millsaps College (Jackson, Mississippi)
- Morehouse College (Atlanta University Center)
- Prescott College (Prescott, Arizona)
- Principia College (Elsah, Illinois)
- St. Louis University (St. Louis, Missouri)
- Spelman College (Atlanta University Center)
- Texas Christian University (Fort Worth, Texas)
- University of Tulsa (Tulsa, Oklahoma)
- Wheaton College (Wheaton, Illinois)

Some schools don't charge students for tuition, in exchange for their working on campus. Here are nine such schools.

- Alice Lloyd College (Pippa Passes, Kentucky)
- Berea College (Berea, Kentucky)
- The Coast Guard Academy (New London, Connecticut; you must serve on active military duty)
- College of the Ozarks (Point Lookout, Missouri)
- Cooper Union (New York City, New York; you must major in architecture, art, or engineering)
- The University of Georgia (Athens; this is for in-state residents only who maintain a B average; the Hope Scholarship program pays their tuition)

- The U.S. Military Academy (West Point, New York; you must serve on active military duty)
- The U.S. Naval Academy (Annapolis, Maryland; you must serve on active military duty)
- The U.S. Air Force Academy (Colorado Springs, Colorado; you must serve on active military duty)

STATE BY STATE

Alabama
Birmingham–Southern College
University of
    Alabama–Tuscaloosa

Alaska
University of Alaska–Fairbanks

Arizona
Prescott College (Prescott)
University of Arizona (Tucson)

Arkansas
Hendrix College (Conway)
University of Arkansas
    (Fayetteville)

California
California Baptist College
    (Riverside)
Deep Springs College (Deep
    Springs)

Colorado
University of
    Colorado–Boulder
The U.S. Air Force Academy

Connecticut
Central Connecticut State
    University (New Britain)
The Coast Guard Academy
    (New London)

Delaware
University of Delaware
    (Newark)

District of Columbia
Howard University
    (Washington, D.C.)

Florida
Florida State University
    (Tallahassee)
New College of the University
    of South Florida (Sarasota)
Stetson University (DeLand)
University of Florida
    (Gainesville)

Georgia
Georgia Institute of
    Technology (Atlanta)
Morehouse College (Atlanta
    U. Center)

Spelman College (Atlanta
U. Center)
University of Georgia (Athens)

Hawaii
Brigham Young University–
Hawaii
University of Hawaii–Manoa

Idaho
Albertson College (Caldwell)

Illinois
DePaul University (Chicago)
Principia College (Elsah)
University of
Illinois–Urbana/Champaign
Wheaton College (Wheaton)

Indiana
Purdue University (West
Lafayette)

Iowa
University of Iowa (Iowa City)

Kansas
University of Kansas
(Lawrence)

Kentucky
Alice Lloyd College (Pippa
Passes)
Berea College (Berea)
Centre College (Danville)

Louisiana
Dillard University (New
Orleans)
Grambling State University
(Grambling)

Northwestern State University
of Louisiana
(Natchitoches)

Maine
University of Maine–Orono

Maryland
St. Mary's College of Maryland
(St. Mary's City)
The U.S. Naval Academy
(Annapolis)

Massachusetts
Gordon College (Wenham)

Michigan
Alma College (Alma)
Calvin College (Grand Rapids)
Hope College (Holland)

Minnesota
Gustavus Adolphus College
(St. Peter)
St. John's University and
College of St. Benedict
(St John's: Collegeville;
St. Benedict: St. Joseph)
University of
Minnesota–Morris
University of Minnesota–Twin
Cities

Mississippi
Millsaps College (Jackson)

Missouri
College of the Ozarks (Point
Lookout)
St. Louis University

Truman State University
(Kirksville)

Montana
Montana Tech of the
University of Montana
(Butte)

Nebraska
University of
Nebraska–Lincoln

Nevada
University of Nevada–Reno

New Hampshire
Keene State College (Keene)

New Jersey
The College of New Jersey
(Ewing)

New Mexico
University of New Mexico
(Albuquerque)

New York
Cooper Union (New York City)
CUNY (City University of New
York)–Brooklyn College
CUNY–City College of New
York
CUNY–Hunter College
CUNY–Queens College
Hofstra University
(Hempstead)
Houghton College (Houghton)
SUNY (State University of New
York)–Binghamton
SUNY–Geneseo

North Carolina
Guilford College (Greensboro)
University of North
Carolina–Asheville
University of North
Carolina–Chapel Hill
University of North
Carolina–Greensboro

North Dakota
Dickinson State University
(Dickinson)
Mayville State University
(Mayville)

Ohio
Miami University (Oxford)
Ohio State University
(Columbus)
University of Dayton

Oklahoma
University of Oklahoma
(Norman)
University of Tulsa

Oregon
University of Oregon (Eugene)

Pennsylvania
Washington and Jefferson
College (Washington)

Rhode Island
Rhode Island College
(Providence)

South Carolina
College of Charleston
Presbyterian College (Clinton)

University of South Carolina (Columbia)
Wofford College (Spartanburg)

South Dakota
Black Hills State University (Spearfish)
Dakota State University (Madison)
Northern State University (Aberdeen)
South Dakota State University (Brookings)

Tennessee
University of Tennessee–Knoxville
University of the South (Sewanee)

Texas
Austin College (Sherman)
Baylor University (Waco)
Rice University (Houston)
Texas Christian University (Fort Worth)
Trinity University (San Antonio)
University of Dallas (Irving)

Utah
Brigham Young University (Provo)

Vermont
Castleton State College (Castleton)

Virginia
College of William and Mary
Mary Washington College
University of Richmond (Virginia)
University of Virginia (Charlottesville)

Washington
Evergreen State College (Olympia)
University of Washington (Seattle)

West Virginia
West Virginia University (Morgantown)

Wisconsin
Alverno College (Milwaukee)
Beloit College (Beloit)
University of Wisconsin–Madison

Wyoming
University of Wyoming (Laramie)

What to Pack

When you think about
packing for school,
what do you think
about? Bringing every-
thing but the kitchen
sink? Bringing every-
thing including the
kitchen sink? Just
remember, you might

**This Can Be True
of Roommates,
Too**

"All the believers were
together and had every-
thing in common. . . .
They gave to anyone as he had need."
(Acts 2:44–45)

have to share a room with someone who also hates to travel light.

The student information packet that your school sends out
when you're accepted will give you suggestions for what to bring.
But what are the essentials—the things you can't do without?

PACKING 101

Use this as your packing checklist. (For some of these items, you
can negotiate with your roommate as to who will bring what.
That way, you can share!)

☑ *Luggage/trunk.* First and foremost, invest in a set of luggage or
a trunk. Your clothes will thank you. (See *Clothes, clothes,
clothes* on next page.)

☑ *Your Bible.* Don't leave home without it!

☑ *A computer and printer.* Handy items for those all-night paper-
writing sessions. Although your school will have computer
labs and a library stocked with computers, it's great to have
one of your own if you can afford it. (Some schools may provide a computer for the room.) A Zip drive or other backup
system is also a nice tool.

❏ *Power strip with surge protector.* If you have a computer or a
number of electrical appliances, this too is a "must-have" item.

☑ *A lamp.* Your room may have good lighting, but a good study
lamp might be necessary.

❏ *A small refrigerator.* You'll need one for munchies. You and your roommate can agree on who brings the fridge.

☑ *A car????* Better check your chosen school's policy. Many schools do not allow freshmen to have cars on campus (but perhaps when you're a sophomore. . .).

❏ *Other transportation items.* You may need a bike to get around campus (don't forget a lock) or in-line skates.

☑ *Clothes, clothes, clothes.* Depending on where your school is located, you might need seasonal items like coats and jackets. If you can go home for the holidays, you won't need to drag a year's supply of clothes with you in the fall. But if you can't get away, be prepared to bring a trunk. (Trunks also make nice tables for a room.) Don't forget a bathrobe.

❏ *Wash and wear.* Most dorms have laundry facilities, but keep in mind that you're competing with fellow students for those washers! You'll need a laundry bag or basket, detergent, a roll of quarters, and plenty of patience.

❏ *Towels.* You *will* need these.

☑ *A clock.* You will need a reliable alarm clock. Can't miss those classes!

☑ *Sheets and a pillow.* Bring two sets of sheets if you can. Don't forget a blanket!

❏ *Iron/small ironing board.* A must for some.

❏ *Sports equipment.* While you may not want to lug skis on your first day, consider the activities you'll be doing regularly. (Ultimate Frisbee anyone?)

☑ *Backpack.* You'll need something in which to carry your books.

☑ *Hangers.* A must. If you have a small space, you might invest in a closet organizer.

❏ *Small first-aid kit.* For emergencies. Include any medicines you have to take and cold medicine/aspirin/ibuprofen.

❏ *Small microwave.* Check with your school's fire safety requirements.

☑ *Small TV.* Not that you'll be looking at this, but you never know.

☑️*Personal hygiene products.* Everything you use daily, bring. Don't forget your shower products: shower shoes, a shower caddy or bucket for carrying your shower products (soap, toothpaste, shampoo). Don't forget the blow-dryer!

❑ *Sewing kit.* You never know when you'll need to repair a rip.

☑️*Mace or pepper spray, whistle.* Check the campus safety requirements.

❑ *Rain gear.* An umbrella or raincoat can be easily stored in a backpack and taken to class.

☑️*Flashlight.* Handy for those late-night hikes from the library or during a brownout.

❑ *A map.* If you're in an unfamiliar city, a map's a great thing to have around. Many maps also have areas of interest you can explore to get to know the city. They also provide public transportation information you'll need to know.

☑️*Your address book/Personal Digital Assistant (PDA)/electronic organizer.* To avoid calling home to get Aunt Millie's phone number, pack your address book or electronic organizer. A Palm Pilot (IBM) is handy for storing hundreds of phone numbers, schedules, and other information. (You can get a Palm Pilot for $350; electronic organizers are about $80.)

❑ *Containers.* Plastic milk crates, Rubbermaid containers, and stackable containers save on space. Milk crates have multiple uses.

☑️*CD player/CDs, earplugs, Walkman.* You know what you like.

☑️*Phone card.* Check with your parents to see if they want to provide you with a phone card, call pack, or whatever they can afford.

❑ *Documents.* You'll need to set up a checking account wherever you go to school, so bring along a Social Security card and/or birth certificate (if necessary), passport, and other documents. You'll also need documentation for school loans. Bring along a box with a lock to store these.

❑ *A throw rug.* Depending on where your school is located, you might find the floors cold in the winter (or early in the morning).

❏ *Paper products.* Paper towels, tissue, plasticware, and paper cups may be necessary. But you can get these when you arrive.

❏ *Bug spray.* You never know!

❏ *Small oscillating fan.* If your room is not air-conditioned (most aren't), your roommate will thank you.

☑ *Small mirror.* Your room may have a dresser mirror, but a small one is handy to have as well.

❏ *Drawer liners/Lysol.* Think of the thousands of students who had your room before you did. Now think of those drawer liners!

❏ *Wall decorations/family photos.* Some dorms don't allow damage to the walls, so you'll need the adhesive-type hooks that stick on the walls. (The residue can sometimes be difficult to remove, however.)

❏ *Office supplies.* A stapler, staples, staple remover, small portable file cabinet, stationery, and printer paper are also useful.

❏ *Other items.* Some people use a fishnet to store things in small rooms. Check with your roommate for room aesthetics.

Keep in mind also that most schools have fire inspections. During those, the RA (residence assistant) inspects your room for fire safety violations. Consequently, hot pots and other appliances that could start a fire if left untended are usually not allowed.

Hey. . .aren't you packed yet?

ACT and SAT and Other Stuff

Wondering whether to take the ACT or the SAT? More than likely, you've already taken one or the other. Or maybe you're just wondering why take either. Colleges use these standardized tests to help them judge the can-

Free Advice

"Therefore I tell you, do not worry about your life.... Do not worry about tomorrow." (Matthew 6:25, 34)

DON'T FORGET Good advice when you're worried about test results.

didates for admission. These tests aren't IQ tests, however. They may not even measure how well you did in high school. After all, not all students are good test takers. But if the college to which you're applying requires a test for admission, run—don't walk—to the nearest testing site.

Remember this: If you don't like your score, most schools will allow you to retake the test and submit your higher score!

THE NAME OF THE GAME

Some midwestern and southern colleges used to prefer the ACT, while the northeastern colleges prefer the SAT. Now many schools accept the ACT or the SAT.

Tips for Any Test

Have more than one # 2 pencil available.
Follow the directions.
Fill in the circles care-fully. (It's easy to make a mistake.)

CATCH A CLUE

Answer the easy questions first.
Circle the questions you don't know, then move on. If you have time, come back to those.
A guess is sometimes better than no answer at all. (The SAT test *does* have a penalty for guessing incorrectly.)

The ACT, published by American College Testing, measures apti-tude in English, mathe-matics, reading, and science. While vocabu-lary isn't emphasized, science and trigonometry are. But don't let that scare you!

The acronym SAT used to mean Scholastic Aptitude Test.

Now the letters stand for Scholastic Assessment Test. There are two SAT tests: SAT I and SAT II. The SAT I tests verbal and math skills. The SAT II (Subject Test) used to be known as the Achievement Test. This test measures what you know about a specific subject like English, foreign languages, math, history, or chemistry. If you've taken the PSATs (Preliminary Scholastic Assessment Test/National Merit Scholarship Qualifying Test), you have an idea of what the SATs are like. The PSATs are taken in the tenth or eleventh grade to prepare a student for the SATs.

Based on your SAT score, a college can know whether you'd do well academically. If you score high in English or any other Subject Test, that can enable you to skip introductory courses. The top colleges require a score of 600–800 in the math and verbal sections of the SAT.

The best rule of thumb when deciding on which SAT II test to take is to choose a subject you know you're good at. Check with the school's admission policy first, however. A school might require that you take a particular Subject Test.

How Much???

SCHOOL COSTS

The important thing to consider when thinking about a college is how much your family can afford. Many financial aid offices use your parents' income to decide how much aid to give you. Your

THE BOTTOM LINE

All You Need

"Do not be anxious about anything, but in everything, by prayer and petition, with thanksgiving, present your requests to God." (Philippians 4:6) That includes your need for financial assistance.

local library can be your best friend for locating financial aid services. Listed below are just a few avenues for aid.

GRANTS AND SCHOLARSHIPS

Many grants are dependent on a student's grades or financial need. Grants do not have to be repaid. (See the Pell Grants under

"Federal Financial Aid" below.) Check with your state financial aid office for in-state grant opportunities.

The Internet is a great place to search for scholarship information. Check out the scholarship database at the web site of the National Association of Student Financial Aid Administrators (NASFAA): www.finaid.org/NASFAA. There are other web sites that offer opportunities to win scholarships or just to find out about them.

- www.collegenet.com
- www.kaplan.com
- www.usnews.com
- www.wgoh.com

Beware though! The Federal Trade Commission (FTC) launched a program in 1996 called "Project $cholar$cam" to warn students about companies offering bogus scholarships. Contact: www.ftc.gov/bcp/conline/pubs/scholarship/index.htm for more information.

Organizations like the Educational Communications Scholarship Foundation also offer scholarships. Contact them at 721 North McKinley Road, P. O. Box 5012, Lake Forest, IL 60045-5012 or 1-847-295-3972. You can request an application from this organization at www.scholar31@ecsf.org.

FEDERAL FINANCIAL AID

All of the grants or loans may sound like so much alphabet soup, but it'll be worth your while to try for them. The Expected Family Contribution (EFC) is the amount used to determine whether you're eligible for Federal Pell Grants, Federal Stafford Loans, Federal Supplemental Educational Opportunity Grants (FSEOG), the Federal Work-Study Program, and Federal Perkins Loans.

Pell Grants. Pell Grants are the largest federal need-based program. About four million Pell Grants are given out. You're almost guaranteed a Pell Grant if your EFC is equal to or less than $2,800. (Pell Grant information: 1-301-722-9200.)

Stafford and FSEOG Loans. Stafford Loans are the largest federal loan program. These loans are both subsidized and unsubsidized. *Subsidized loans* means that the government pays the interest until the repayment period starts. For a Stafford Loan, you'll need to be eligible for a Pell Grant. In order to try for an FSEOG, you need to be eligible for a Pell Grant and have exceptional financial need. Contact your state agency for Stafford Loan information.

Federal Perkins Loans. To apply for this type of loan, you have to go through the financial aid office of your chosen school. That school also sets the deadline for application.

Direct Loans and FFEL. You can also apply for the Federal Direct Student Loan Program and the Federal Family Education Loan Program (FFEL). These loans are also both subsidized and unsubsidized. Direct loans are disbursed through your school. After the money is paid for tuition and room and board, leftover money is given to you by check. You can decide on a number of repayment plans. The Direct Loan Program and FFEL Program Loans for Parents (also known as the PLUS Loan—Parent Loans for Undergraduate Students) allows your parents to borrow money to pay for your college expenses.

Federal Work-Study Program. Work-Study programs provide jobs on campus and off for eligible students. Usually students work 10–20 hours per week. There may be a yearly cap on how much you can earn.

Your family will need to fill out an FAFSA (Free Application for Federal Student Aid) for any federal assistance. Check an on-line service like www.collegenet.com for an application. Applications must be mailed to Application for Federal Student Aid, Federal Student Aid Programs, Box 4001, Mt. Vernon, Illinois 62864-8601; 1-319-337-5665. Better file early, though (anytime after January 1)!

Check out the College Scholarship Service (CSS) for help in analyzing your family's need. You'll need to fill in a CSS/Financial Aid Profile. (Contact College Scholarship Service, P. O. Box 6920, Princeton, New Jersey 08541-6920 [1-609-771-7735].) Call the Federal Student Financial Aid Information Center at 1-800-4FED-AID (1-800-433-3243) if you have questions about a particular school or about federal financial aid. You can also call the Kaplan Student Loan Information Program at 1-888-KAP-LOAN for loan information.

OTHER AVENUES

Sallie Mae, Nellie Mae, The Education Resources Institute (TERI), and EduCap Inc. are organizations that offer loans or loan consolidation. Sallie Mae: www.Salliemae.com or 1-800-FAA-7562. Nellie Mae: 50 Braintree Hill Park; Braintree, Massachusetts 02184-9916; 1-800-852-0603.

The National and Community Service Program is another student work program. Write to The Corporation for National and Community Service, 1100 Vermont Avenue, NW, Washington, D.C. 20525 (1-800-942-2677).

STATE FINANCIAL AID

Each state has its own agency for financial aid. Your high school guidance counselor can help you find the agency you need. A book like Barron's *Complete College Financing Guide* by Marguerite Dennis (New York: Barron's Educational Series, Inc.) has lists of state agencies and their numbers. Your local library should have a copy for the most current year.

CATCH A CLUE

Scholarships for Minority Students

Many private foundations and organizations offer scholarships. Below are some organizations that offer aid.
Bureau of Indian Affairs Higher Education Grant Program. **Eligible Native American students can contact The Bureau of Indian Affairs, 18th and C Streets, NW, Washington, D.C. 20245.**

Congressional Hispanic Caucus. **Qualified Hispanic students can contact Congressional Hispanic Caucus, 504 C Street, NE, Washington, D.C. 20002.**

General Motors Scholarship Program. **This corporation offers scholarships to minority undergraduate students. Contact General Motors Scholarship Program, c/o General Motors Corporation, 8-163 General Motors Building, Detroit, Michigan 48202.**

The United Negro College Fund. **Over 1,000 scholarships are awarded yearly. To be eligible, you must attend a United Negro College Fund school. Contact the United Negro College Fund, Inc., 8260 Willow Oaks Corporate Drive, Fairfax, Virginia 22031; 1-800-331-2244.**

THE COLLEGE'S FINANCIAL AID

All schools offer aid of some type to needy students. Check with the financial aid director of your chosen school for eligibility.

VETERANS PROGRAMS

Many of these programs involve service in the armed forces for a required amount of time.

ROTC Scholarship Program. Students with these scholarships have to serve four years in the Army, Navy, Air Force, or Marines after graduating

CATCH A CLUE

Application Fees

In addition to tuition costs, room and board, and books, don't forget the first payment you need to make: the application fee for the school of your choice. Check the school's admissions office for applicable application fees.

from college. They remain on reserve duty another two years.

Service Academy Scholarships. Students enrolling in military academies are qualified for these scholarships. The only catch is you must be nominated by your U.S. senator or representative.

Financial Assistance Programs for Military. Each branch of the service offers programs. See your recruitment office for more details.

Montgomery GI Bill. The government provides money monthly for education. To be eligible a person has to serve at least two years. The money allotment increases after three years of service.

FINANCIAL AID FOR THE HANDICAPPED

Here are just a few.

American Foundation for the Blind. Contact the American Foundation for the Blind, 15 W. 16th Street, New York, New York 10011.

Alexander Graham Bell Association for the Deaf. Contact the Alexander Graham Bell Association for the Deaf, 3417 Volta Place, NW, Washington D.C. 20007-2778.

Disabled American Veterans Auxiliary National Education Loan Fund. Contact the National Education Loan Fund Director, National Headquarters, Disabled American Veterans Auxiliary, 3725 Alexandria Pike, Cold Spring, Kentucky 41076.

Section 2
Major Problems

Choosing a Major

WHAT WILL YOU BE?

As a kid you were asked, "What do you want to be when you grow up?" As you consider a major, you need to take that question further: "How can this major help me *toward* that goal?" This is the time to really be in prayer about what you want to accomplish during your college years.

MAJOR QUESTIONS

What Is a Major?

This is a group of related courses within a field of study. Accounting, biblical languages, English, political science—each is a major. Usually a student is required to choose an official major by his or her sophomore or junior year. (Premed and engineering students, however, declare their intent earlier, due to course requirements.) Each college usually

CATCH A CLUE

Choosing a Major

A story on choosing a major:
I'm majoring in literature. I was a music major beforehand. I got really frustrated with it. I found myself not liking it very much. I thought, *Hey? What else can I major in?* So I thought of movies and literature. I had two really good literature classes in high school. I thought, *That'll be a fun major.* It's given me a lot of time to fellowship with my friends, to be involved with my church and the music groups here [at the college], and the accountability groups. It helps me understand how people communicate. I really think that's important.—Andy, Naperville, IL

has specific requirements for graduation. These include the number of course credits needed to graduate and the distribution requirements. Distribution requirements (sometimes called *general education requirements*) are those classes outside of your major that a college requires for graduation. For example, you may need to take a math or foreign language course. Most colleges also require freshman composition, unless you test out of that. Check your school's catalog for courses you can take that are related to your major *(cognates)*.

What Is a Student-Designed (Ad Hoc) Major?

Suppose the program offered by a major doesn't quite give you all that you want. What could you do? You might construct your own program of study with the help of an advisor. Your course of study must be approved by the college, however.

To Each Their Own

"God has given each of us the ability to do certain things well." (Romans 12:6 NLT)

THE BIBLE SAYS

What Is an Independent Study?

This program allows you to work on a subject independently. Instead of going to class, you would meet regularly with an academic advisor, who checks your progress. A final project is usually required for a grade. Many students do independent studies during their senior year. Some majors require independent studies. For example, a student majoring in English at Northwestern University had to turn in a 20-page paper as the final project for her independent study. She met with her advisor once a week.

What Is the Study Abroad Program?

This program allows you to—what else—study abroad. Many students, particularly those majoring in a foreign language, live and attend classes in a country for a semester or a year to soak in the language and culture and to minister there.

QUESTIONS TO ASK YOUR SCHOOL ABOUT MAJORS

• Approximately how many students have this major?

• What campus job opportunities are there for students in this major?

• What is recruitment like for this major?

• What percentage of students with this major go on to grad school?

MAJOR CHANGES

Keep in mind that you *can* change your mind about a major. Even though you might have written *chemical engineering* on your application, you're not locked in

Relatively Speaking

"If I had to live my life over again, I would elect to be a trader of goods rather than a student of science. I think barter is a noble thing."
—Albert Einstein

WOW!

to that major forever. Many students experiment with different majors as they search for the one that fits them the best. But consider the time factor. If you've already invested a lot of time in say English literature and you want to switch to electrical engineering, you may be in for some extra *years* at school. Consider also the types of courses offered in a major. Some sequence courses are offered only once a year. If you miss (or fail) the first course, you have to wait a whole year before you can take that course again.

MAJOR HELP

If you need help to decide on a major, where can you go?

Your High School Counselor
This person can help you understand how your academic performance thus far has prepared you to handle a particular major.

Your Parents
They want you to succeed in life. If you're really undecided, ask what your gifts and talents are. Ask them what they think God's plan might be for your future.

Your School's Course Catalog
It has answers. Really.

Your Academic Advisor
This person is assigned to help you choose the courses you need and to make sure you fulfill the distribution requirements. Keep in mind that your academic advisor is a busy person. You will need to seek him or her out. Be persistent in getting the information you need.

WIDE ANGLE

Major Decisions

Yes, choosing a major is an important decision, just as important as choosing a college. In high school, you were pretty much told what to take. As an adult, the choice is yours. Here are some questions to consider as you think about a major.

What career or life goal will you pursue? How will this major help?
How interested are you in this subject? Circle your interest level.

1	2	3	4	5	6	7	8	9	10
Not at all interested				*Moderately interested*				*Very interested*	

How do your talents and abilities fit this major?
If you took classes in this subject in high school, how well did you do?
Are there prerequisites for this major? (A *prerequisite* is a requirement to qualify for a class or major. For example, if calculus is a prerequisite and your last math class was algebra, better quickly sign up for math tutoring! It's best to get prerequisites out of the way during your first or second year because you'll be busy enough with your major classes later.)

1	2	3	4	5	6	7	8	9	10
Not at all interested				*Moderately interested*				*Very interested*	

How dedicated will you be to this major?
Is grad school or a professional school (law, medical, or dental school) necessary for future employment?

1	2	3	4	5	6	7	8	9	10
Not at all interested				*Moderately interested*				*Very interested*	

An Academic Dean

A dean can also help you understand the requirements of a major, particularly if you're thinking about switching from one department to another. This person is usually extremely busy, so make an appointment.

A Professor You've Gotten to Know

If you've taken a class that resonates with you, talk with the professor about the requirements of the major. Ask him or her about his or her own undergraduate years.

A Student Who Has (or Had) This Major

Many colleges place freshmen with roommates who have the same major or are in the same college in a university. Talk with your roommate or a friend about his or her struggles with a major. Talk to some third- and fourth-year students and alumni as well. Ask questions about the class workload.

Aptitude Tests

Some companies like CFKR Career Materials (1-800-525-5626) offer aptitude tests to help you learn what you're good at. The Major-Minor Finder is the test offered by CFKR. Check with your counselor about whether an aptitude test is right for you.

MAJOR RESOURCES

Check out www.collegeedge.com for advice on choosing majors. "Major Advice and Information" provides excellent tips to help you select a major. "The Inside Scoop on Majors" has interviews with students in ten of the most popular majors. They describe how much work is involved in each major. See also the University of Pennsylvania's web site (www.sas.upenn.edu/college/major/major_overview.html). Even if you're not planning to apply to the University of Pennsylvania, the site provides general tips you can use when choosing a major.

Minoring in the Majors

MAJOR "LITE"

Want to make the most of your college education? Then think about a minor. A minor is a group of related courses with fewer required credits than a major. In other words, you

THE BIBLE SAYS

You've a Lot to Explore

"Now there are different kinds of spiritual gifts, but it is the same Holy Spirit who is the source of them all. There are different kinds of service in the church, but it is the same Lord we are serving. There are different ways God works in our lives, but it is the same God who does the work through all of us. A spiritual gift is given to each of us as a means of helping the entire church." (1 Corinthians 12:4–7 NLT)

get the experience of another major with half the courses. Your minor could be within the same department as your major or in a different area. For example, one English major decided to minor in psychology. Both her major and minor were part of the same college (Arts and Sciences) within her university. This student felt that the study of human psychology would be an asset to her writing.

A minor helps you get your feet wet in other subjects. A minor could also help you discover a profession or ministry you never considered before or help you specialize in a particular field. For example, one premed student with a psychology minor as an undergraduate decided to pursue psychiatry as a resident.

Do I need a minor? you might ask. That depends on what your school requires. A minor can be attractive to future employers and grad schools. You don't have to stick with just one minor, however. You can go for more than one if you've got the time, or go for a double major. (See "Considering a Double Major.") Consider a subject that works with your major or one in which you have a strong interest.

See whether your chosen college offers the option of declaring a minor. Check the school's catalog for the exact requirements. If there are prerequisites, you can get those taken care of during your first or second year. Your school might also offer specific minors. For example at LeTourneau University, biology, chemistry, physical education, and physics are offered as minors in the natural sciences and physical education department. Your school's catalog can provide more details.

SOME "MINOR" DETAILS

Here are some questions to consider when thinking about a minor.

- Which subject will you pursue as a minor? Why?
- How does it relate to your major?
- How will it help you achieve your life's goal?
- How does it tie in with your gifts or abilities?
- Are there prerequisites? If so, what are they?

- Are there prerequisites that overlap with your chosen major? Which ones?

- Does your chosen college require that you declare a minor? If so, what are the requirements of declaring a minor?

Considering a Double Major

TWO FOR THE PRICE OF ONE

Want to send your college education into warp drive? Go for the double-header—a double major. A double major means you've met the requirements for two majors. For example, a recent graduate of the University

THE BIBLE SAYS

Be Like Paul: Study Hard

"Under Gamaliel I was thoroughly trained in the law of our fathers and was just as zealous for God as any of you are today." (Acts 22:3)

of Iowa had a double major of English literature (with an emphasis on women authors) and fine arts (summa cum laude no less!).

Insane, you say? Not really. Some students consider a double major to be a smart investment. One ambitious student, interviewed on the Internet, had a double major in biochemistry and physics. Another student at a university graduated with two engineering degrees. She was promptly pursued by several major corporations. Still another student majored in organ performance and church music—a natural combination.

WIDE ANGLE

Resources

Check out *Choose a Christian College* (Princeton, New Jersey: Peterson's Guides, Inc./Christian College Coalition; get the current year's guide) for more help in finding a major that fits.

Shaheena Ahmad gives practical advice for double majors in *The Yale Daily News Guide to Succeeding in College*. It's practical because Ahmad herself had a double major in English and political science at Yale.

MAJOR TIPS

A double major isn't for everyone. If you sense that your workload will already be tough enough, don't feel obligated. Or, consider a minor (see "Minoring in the Majors").

If you decide to double major, try to find two majors that go well together. Believe it or not, physics and biochemistry go well together because of the core of classes both draw upon. Once you decide what to major in, take care of your distribution requirements early. For example, if you know that you have a math or foreign language requirement, you'll want to get that out of the way. If necessary, take a course at another college during the summer. Check beforehand to see whether your school will accept the course credit.

The chart below can help you consider the plusses and minuses of double majoring.

CATCH A CLUE

Plusses and Minuses

Plusses for Double Majoring

- You gain skills in two different areas of study.
- You gain the value of two majors for the price of one.
- You won't have regrets about what you could have majored in.
- You gain a more impressive résumé and transcript.

Minuses for Double Majoring

- You have to make doubly sure all requirements are met.
- You may have to take a full course load for four years and perhaps an extra semester or attend summer school.
- You don't get to take a variety of classes because all of your time is spent in the two concentrations.

What You Really Need

THE BOTTOM LINE

Paul was trained by the most respected rabbi of his day. That meant that Paul was very well educated. But even Paul would admit that with all his training, he was still wrong about the Son of God—that is until the Damascus Road incident. (See Acts 9:1–9.) After that, he was able to take what he learned and use it for God's glory. An education that does not enhance an appreciation for God and His creation will not be helpful to you, even if you gain fifty college degrees. As Jesus said, "What good will it be for a man if he gains the whole world, yet forfeits his soul? Or what can a man give in exchange for his soul?" (Matthew 16:26). How will you use what you learn for God's glory?

Check your school's catalog for the requirements and restrictions of double majors. Some schools may require that your double major involve a B.A. and a B.S., rather than two B.A.s. Then make an appointment to talk with your academic advisor and the deans of your college about double majoring. See if they can recommend a student who chose the same double major. If so, talk with that person about his or her workload. Ask plenty of questions!

The Majors and Your Future

YOUR LIFE GOAL

"Times, they are a changin' " according to the popular song. In years past, a graduate degree was not necessary for many careers. Today, however, the sheer volume of

Aim High

CATCH A CLUE

"Don't let anyone look down on you because you are young, but set an example for the believers in speech, in life, in love, in faith and in purity." (I Timothy 4:12)

qualified applicants makes a graduate degree a necessity for many jobs. As you consider the list of majors below, prayerfully consider what you need to do to achieve your life's goal.

- *Accounting*. To be a CPA or not to be a CPA? That is the question. Accounting courses will train you for a job in public or managerial accounting. But to be a CPA, you will need to be licensed. An undergraduate accounting degree does gain you general experience in economics, finance, and business law. To specialize, you'll have to go to grad school.

- *Advertising*. The experience you gain can lead to a copywriting job. This is a very competitive field, however. To be an account executive, you may need a master's degree in advertising.

The Future and You

The British sometimes say "youth at the helm" when talking about a young person in a leadership role. College prepares you today for future leadership roles tomorrow.

WOW!

- *Aerospace engineering/science*. A program like the Aerospace Science program at LeTourneau University (Longview, Texas) prepares students to be commercial pilots, flight instructors, or other types of aviation professionals. Students would have clocked approximately 250 hours of flight training and have earned a Commercial Pilot Certificate with an Instrument Rating and Certified Flight Instructor Certificate. Missionary aviation is encouraged, since the Commercial Pilot Certificate with Instrument Rating is required by mission boards (not to mention the AP Mechanic Certificate). The experience you gain can lead to a job. For research and development jobs, however, get ready for grad school. Ah, ah, ah. No buts.

- *African-American, Hispanic, Native American, or women's studies*. Many people majoring in ethnic or area studies plan to teach or go on to a professional career. That will mean grad school. The interdisciplinary nature of the program allows a student to study a broad range of subjects (history, literature, anthropology).

- *Anthropology/geography/political science, and so on*. With social science degrees like archaeology, anthropology, economics, and political science, you need to have a plan for your postgraduate years. Law school? Graduate work? A Ph.D. or J.D. (Juris Doctor—a law degree) may be in your future.

- *Art/fine arts/history/therapy/graphic arts*. There are many different avenues: museum curator, art therapy, a professional career as an artist, and so on. The increase in art students shows the popularity and competitiveness of the field. An M.F.A. (Master of Fine Arts) might give you the edge.

- *Astronomy/chemistry/physics*. Think: grad school. Some jobs require a master's degree at the very least, or a Ph.D. For chemistry, ACS (American Chemical Society) certification is a plus for employment.

- *Biblical languages/studies*. You'll gain a good background in the study of Greek, Hebrew, and the Old and New Testaments as an undergraduate, but be prepared to head to the nearest seminary afterward. Some graduates with B.A.s do find work in Christian publishing.

- *Biology/biological science/biochemistry*. You can't pass GO without thinking of grad school.

- *Broadcasting*. Entry-level jobs can still be had, but keep in mind the sheer competitiveness of this field. Some companies consider the school you attend as the deciding point. Others consider the experience gained through internships. This is a field that may require working your way up from the bottom.

- *Business administration/commerce management*. You'll learn the basics of business operation and management as an undergrad. An M.B.A. may be necessary because of the competitiveness of the field.

- *Civil engineering*. This major can gain you some entry-level jobs with major corporations. A master's degree may be a necessity for some entry-level positions, however.

- *Communications*. This broad course of study gives you an overview of different media. You might consider a concentration like advertising, journalism, or public relations if you know specifically what you'd like to do.

- *Computer information systems/programming science*. The computer industry has grown astronomically. When you think future, think computers.

- *Creative writing*. If you want to be a writer, this major will only take you so far. Sheer talent, grit, and determination will take you the rest of the way.

- *Education*. This major prepares you for certification. Students decide whether to concentrate on early childhood, elementary, or secondary teaching. Student teaching is a must. You must go to grad school to teach at the college level. (Some schools may require grad school for secondary positions.)

- *English*. Will you teach? Will you write? Your decision can push you into grad school or into an entry-level editorial job.

- *Film studies*. The film industry is an extremely competitive field, so think film school or get to know Steven Spielberg. A program like the Los Angeles Film Studies Center, started by the Christian College Coalition, can help you learn what it's like to be a Christian in the film industry. This program offers non-paying internships.

- *Finance/banking*. Course work can prepare you for an entry-level position. But consider grad school for a Master of Finance degree or an M.B.A.

- *French/Spanish/German*. Foreign languages are helpful for missionaries and those who wish to teach at the high school level. But if you have no idea what you want to do, majoring in a language may be a detriment in job hunting.

- *History*. Majoring in history can give you a background for teaching history or for law school. Graduate work is encouraged for some professions.

- *Journalism*. This major can prepare you for newspaper or magazine reporting, thanks to the internships built into the programs of many colleges. The field is very competitive, however. Consider attending a school that is well-known for this major (for example, Northwestern University).

- *(Pre)law sequence*. Courses will take you to the LSAT and on to law school. This is a very competitive field, however, because of the recent glut in lawyers. (Insert your favorite lawyer joke here.)

- *Marketing/retailing/merchandising*. This major provides a broad overview of the sale and promotion of goods. Many major in marketing, but jobs aren't always easy to come by. An M.B.A. is encouraged for many jobs.

- *Mathematics*. The math and computer-science major is popular because the two go hand in hand. There are many opportunities for mathematicians because of a decline in mathematicians in recent years. Math is not a major for the squeamish.

- *(Pre)medicine sequence*. Course work will take you to the MCAT and on to medical school. This is a very competitive field. Some courses are designed to weed out premed students.

- *Ministries*. This is a broad field of study that can prepare you for a leadership role in a church. That goal will take you to seminary.

Success Is. . .

A good school + a good program in your major = a good education.

DON'T FORGET

- *Missions*. There is no better "field" of study than the mission field after you graduate.

- *Music education*. Teacher certification or grad school beckons. Recent cutbacks in music education within the public school system is a point to consider.

- *Music performance*. Performance majors can be competitive and rigorous. You must be dedicated.

- *Nursing*. This major provides excellent hands-on training. Nurses are always needed.

- *Philosophy*. If you wish to teach, grad school is a must. If you're not certain what to do with a philosophy degree, run—don't walk—to the nearest academic advisor.

- *Political science/government*. If you want to be an attorney, get ready for law school. If you want to teach or go into politics, get ready for grad school or get to know your state senator. Internships can assist you in getting into a good law school or grad school.

- *Psychology*. Grad school is required before you can even think about getting a job. Undergraduate course work just whets your whistle for grad school.

- *Public relations*. Through this major, you will learn to communicate a client's interests. Entry-level jobs can be had, but these are not always easy to come by. (This major may fall under the communications umbrella of study.)

- *Radio and television studies*. This is a very hands-on major if you're considering work in the radio/television industry. Entry-level jobs can be had, but internships are an absolute must.

- *Reading education*. Think: grad school or teacher certification. Reading specialists are in demand in public schools and in educational publishing.

- *Religious education/studies*. Think about what you want to do. (Write curriculum? Be a Sunday school superintendent? Teach at the college level?) Course work in other disciplines (journalism/writing) or a seminary degree might be necessary.

- *Social work*. This major provides a social sciences overview and an emphasis on human behavior. A master's degree is a requirement for many jobs.

- *Special education*. A master's degree is a requirement for many jobs.

- *Speech pathology and audiology*. Two words: grad school. You *will* need a master's degree to get a job.

- *Technical writing*. Jobs are plentiful, thanks to the computer industry.

- *Theater arts/drama*. An extremely competitive field where talent and/or "who you know" counts.

- *Theology*. Think: grad school. This major can provide a background for an entry-level job in a Christian publishing company.

- *Voice*. A very competitive field. For an operatic career, you will need to work with a known voice teacher and be tops at your school. Not too difficult, right?

- *Youth ministries*. To be a youth pastor or a D.C.E., think seminary. To be an editor at a Christian publishing company, think internship during your undergrad years and course work in journalism or creative writing.

- *Zoology*. Run—don't walk—to the nearest grad school if you want to be a zoologist. A bachelor's degree can get you a job as a research assistant or allow you to teach in a high school.

Section 3

Roommate Roulette

Getting Along with Your Roommate

So. . .you're about to get a roommate. And you feel good about it. *Should be fun,* you think. *I've shared a room with my brother, so I'm used to this.* Or, *I'm rooming with my best friend from high*

CATCH A CLUE

A Good Roommate

"As iron sharpens iron, so one man [a roommate!] sharpens another."
(Proverbs 27:17)

school. No problem, this will be smooooooth sailing. But maybe that's not you. Perhaps you're feeling a little less confident. You've never had to share a room with anyone, or you're getting ready to move in with a total and complete stranger. What if she hates you? What if he's a total jerk? Either way, there are some important things to keep in mind.

First, you've got to remember that your roommate was created special by God, just the way he is. No matter what happens, keep looking for those good qualities. On the other hand, don't forget that he's human—just like you are. Neither one of you will naturally be "the perfect" roommate. Leave each other room to make mistakes. Don't forget that God put you two together for a reason. Maybe it's to make you best friends, maybe it's to teach you how to love someone who's hard to love. Either way, you can trust God to use this for your good!

ROOMMATE ETIQUETTE

Don't:

- Move your stuff in and take over beds, dressers, closet space, etc., before your roommate gets there—unless you've talked to her first. You might think you're doing a nice thing by leaving her the top bunk, but what if it turns out she has a phobia about heights?

- Feel like you have to be best friends—especially right away. There's no need to put that kind of pressure on you or your roommate. Maybe you will be eventually, maybe not—and that's okay. Wait and see what happens as you get to know each other better.

Always Keep This in Mind

"Do to others what you would have them do to you." (Matthew 7:12)

CATCH A CLUE

- Assume your roommate has the same sense of modesty as you do. Just because you feel comfortable walking around in your underwear all the time doesn't mean he'll feel comfortable with it, too.

- Borrow something (especially something intensely personal—like a toothbrush! or something intensely expensive—like a car!) without asking first—unless you've already talked about it and you've been given an unconditional carte blanche to use whatever you want. (But don't hold your breath waiting to get this; don't you have a few things you'd rather no one else used?)

- Wait until you feel as if you're about to explode to talk to your roommate about something that bothers you. Keep short accounts with one another. Deal with problems right away. Who wants to room with Mount Saint Helens?

Do:

- Ask lots of questions. Work at finding out how your roommate feels about all sorts of things—from her pet peeves to her favorite kind of dessert to her views on God. But don't push—everyone has a right to keep certain things to themselves!

- Serve your roommate. Look for ways to ways to show God's love.

- Be willing to compromise. There's no need to major in the minors. Not only is it selfish to expect to always have things your way, it's unrealistic!

- Be patient and forgiving. Even the best of roommates will let you down sometimes. And you can be sure that you'll return the favor someday.

- Pray, pray, pray for your roommate. Make it a point to ask your roommate occasionally how you can best pray for him, and then do it!

Whether you realize it or not, you probably have certain expectations of what life will be like with your roommate. Here's a quiz to test whether your expectations are too high, too low, or just about right.

TEST YOURSELF
1. You figure that you and your roommate will
    A. Discover that you were really twins separated at birth, and you'll want to make up for lost time by spending every waking moment together.
    B. Have a totally different circle of friends and will never see each other at all, and that doesn't bother you a bit.
    C. Spend time together but will also have things that you'll be involved in apart from each other.

2. You expect that you and your roommate will
    A. Fight like cats and dogs, so you've got to either be a doormat or be prepared to do battle.
    B. Be in 100 percent agreement about everything and never disagree.
    C. Experience some measure of conflict that will need to be worked through.

3. A good roommate should
    A. Be willing to share even her deodorant with you, and you won't even have to ask.
    B. Ask before borrowing something and give the other person the freedom to say no.
    C. Use White-Out to paint a line down the middle of the room and not touch the things on the other person's half.
4. I'm sure my roommate will
    A. Sometimes know what I think or feel by looking at me but other times will have to ask or will need me to tell him.

B. Have ESP and be able to read my mind and will know how I feel without my having to say a word.

C. Not care one bit about what's going on with me, and I won't care to tell him.

5. A great roommate is
   A. A myth—there's no such thing.
   B. Someone you can learn to enjoy living with.
   C. A combination of Cinderella's fairy godmother, Daddy Warbucks, Merry Maids, and your favorite golden retriever.

6. The atmosphere in our room/apartment/house
   A. Will depend on what we choose together to make it—peaceful or wild-and-crazy, homey or just a place to sleep, fun or someplace to dread being.
   B. Will probably end up being the exact opposite of what I'd want it to be. (If I'm looking for some fun, it will be like a funeral parlor. If I'm hoping for a quiet place to study, it will be a constant party. . . . You get the idea.)
   C. Will reflect my need at the moment—quiet when I want to study, Disneyland when I want to have fun, cozy and homey when I'm missing my family.

How Did You Score?

1. A. 6	B. 2	C. 4
2. A. 2	B. 6	C. 4
3. A. 6	B. 4	C. 2
4. A. 4	B. 6	C. 2
5. A. 2	B. 4	C. 6
6. A. 4	B. 2	C. 6

How Do Your Expectations Rate?

36–28—Are you kidding?!? You're going to be in for a rude awakening with these kinds of expectations. You need to sit down and rethink what you're looking for, and this time take off the rose-colored glasses.

26–22—You seem to have a good handle on what lies ahead. You expect to find both good and bad and know that you'll have to work to develop the good. With that attitude, you ought to do well with whomever you're rooming with.

20–12—Either you're afraid of being disappointed or your last roommate made Frankenstein look good. Murphy's Law doesn't *always* come true. It's okay to have some sort of positive expectations. If you don't, you'll only see the bad and won't do anything to work on it. Who wants to live like that?

DEALING WITH CONFLICT

Just face it. It's bound to happen. At some point, you and your roommate will experience conflict. It might be the first day, or it might take longer. It might be over something minor, or it could be something major. At any rate, it's inevitable. So, what do you do when it happens? Pack up and move out? You'll find yourself moving a lot if you do! For starters, you can think through the "Conflict Survey."

WOW!

The Roommate from Next Door

I'd spent all day traveling 2,000 miles and arrived at my dorm room at 4 P.M. My roommate, who I'd only talked to on the phone once, grew up just down the street from the college and had been moving her "stuff" in since 8 A.M. And man, did she have a lot of stuff. It was everywhere! It was obvious where my bed and desk were; they were the only things not completely submerged beneath a mountain of stuff. Even the walls were covered—with magazine clippings of scantily clothed models and posters of bare-chested men. Led Zeppelin blared from her tape player. Yikes! Not exactly my idea of the perfect roommate. Hoping to escape for a moment, I went straight to the bathroom. I sat down on the toilet to catch my breath, and looked up thinking, "Lord, what am I doing here?" Well, I didn't see God up there, but I did see a poster of Tom Cruise—staring down at me from the bathroom ceiling! Oh, brother. There appeared to be no escape. So I decided I'd better smile and go make friends, first with Tom, then with my roommate. It could have been worse, I suppose. At least it was Tom Cruise on the ceiling and not Led Zeppelin.—Raeanna, Los Alamitos, CA

CONFLICT SURVEY: QUESTIONS TO ASK YOURSELF WHEN CONFLICT ARISES

1. What exactly is the problem? (Try to boil the answer down to one sentence. This will help force you to get to the heart of the matter.)

2. Why does this bother me? Am I just being selfish? Is it because I'm concerned for my roommate and our relationship?

3. Has this happened before with my roommate? If so, when and how often? How did I deal with it last time? Was that effective?

4. Does this fit best under the category of "pet peeves," "relational issues," "moral issues," or _____ (fill in the blank)?

5. On a scale of 1 to 10 (10 being extremely important), how important is this issue to me?

6. Are there other issues that we need to deal with that are more important right now?

7. If I could have the ideal situation in regard to this issue, what would it look like? Is this realistic to hope for, or am I asking too much?

Thinking through these questions will help you evaluate what's going on and begin to figure out what to do about it. It's important to be sure you really understand the problem. Maybe your roommate borrowed a piece of paper without asking, and you're still burning up about it. A piece of paper is not a big deal, so why are you so mad? Perhaps your roommate has borrowed other things—bigger things—without asking, and you never told her it upset you. If that's the case, you're dealing with more than just the paper, and you need to realize that.

Knowing that not all conflict is in the same category, it helps to figure out where yours falls. You'll need to deal with a moral issue much differently than a pet peeve. Some things, once you think through them, really aren't a big deal, and you'll realize you just need to put some of your own self-ishness aside. But other things are worth talking about, especially if it's only going to get worse, and it's important that you not sweep those under the rug. Deal with them! And don't wait until two months later after it's happened another five times and you're so mad you feel like you're going to burst.

And one more thing, be sure that you have a clear idea of what you're hoping for. If you're clear on the changes you'd like to see, it will make it much easier to explain them to her.

CATCH A CLUE

Tips for When You Talk to Your Roommate about the Problem

Pick the right place and the right time. Don't do it when one of you is tired or upset, and don't do it where other people might hear or interrupt you.

Start off with positive things. Tell your roommate some of the things you like about her and about living with her. She'll be more likely to really hear what you have to say about the issue at hand.

If your roommate is going to be upset by what you have to say, or you think he might jump to certain conclusions, be sure to tell him those things. Voice your fears. It's better to have them out in the open.

Use "I" and "me" statements. Don't say things like, "*You* make me so mad because *you always* borrow things without asking." Instead, try saying, "It upsets *me* when you borrow my things without asking because *I* feel like *I'm* not being shown respect." The first way will make your roommate feel like you're on the attack and she'll be more likely to get defensive and not really hear you.

WHAT AND WHEN TO SHARE

Obviously, you're going to have to share some things—like the air you breathe. And you're going to have some things you don't want to share. You and your roommate will have to work out which things are okay and which ones are off-limits. Use the following checklist as a tool for discussing with your roommate how each of you feels about sharing certain types of things. For each item on the checklist, answer these questions.

Do I need to ask first? What if the other person isn't around to be asked? You may also discuss alternatives, such as leaving a note to let the other person know you borrowed something.

How much is too much? You might be fine letting your roommate use your car every once in awhile, but you don't want her having access to it every day. Or, it wouldn't bother you if he used your computer, but if you needed to use it, then you want to have the right to kick him off.

What if I use it all up (as in toiletries) or it breaks while I'm using it (such as a computer)? Knowing what to expect if this happens will keep you from conflict later, and you might decide it's not worth the liability to borrow it in the first place.

Sharing Checklist

Check off the boxes after you and your roommate have discussed how each of you feels about sharing.

❏ Clothing—including shoes, outfits, coats, and that favorite junior high outfit you just can't bear to part with

❏ Personal/toiletry items—like shampoo, toothpaste, hair spray, or earwax solvent

❏ Books—including textbooks, leisure reading, personal diaries, and your latest copy of *Ranger Rick* magazine

❏ Small appliances—like a hair dryer, iron, toaster oven, or ham radio for contacting life on other planets

❏ Major electronics—such as a computer, stereo, microwave, or portable foot massager

❏ Car—not only the issue of borrowing the car but also to what extent you're willing to chauffeur the other person around

DEALING WITH A ROOMMATE'S DEPRESSION OR HABITS

At some point during college, you may find yourself with a roommate who has some truly serious problems. Learning to recognize these problems and knowing what to do about them can make a huge difference in her life and yours. If you suspect that your roommate has an eating disorder, is addicted to drugs or alcohol, is suffering from depression or perhaps even contemplating suicide, she needs more help than you can give her. There are places you can get that help. If you live in the dorms, you can speak to your RA or the resident director of your dorm. Or you might consider speaking with the dean of students. Many schools also have some sort of counseling center where you should be able to find assistance. The bottom line is that you need to take the problem to someone who has been trained to deal with it; don't try to deal with it by yourself. Even if you think your roommate will hate you for talking to someone else about what's going on, for her sake, you need to do it. It could very well be a matter of life and death.

The following gives specific issues as well as hot lines or organizations you might call for more information or for help.

• Anorexia and bulimia—*American Anorexia/Bulimia Assoc.* 1-212-575-6200

• Suicide—*The Hope Line* 1-800-394-4673 (evenings only)

• Alcoholism—*Alanon* 1-800-245-4546

• Drug addiction—*National Teen Challenge* 1-800-814-5729

• Crisis pregnancy—*Bethany Lifeline* 1-800-BETHANY

How to Choose a Great Roommate

MAKING A GOOD CHOICE

So, you didn't have a choice the first time you got a roommate. Or maybe you did, but you realized you didn't make a very *good* choice. How can you do better? First, you can ask yourself what you've learned from any past roommate experiences. What things are important to you, and what things aren't such a big deal? What were the things you enjoyed about your previous roommate, and what things were hard to live with? What do you hope to be different next time around?

Next, use the "Qualities Spectrum" to think through who might be a good match for you. This will help you evaluate various qualities and compare how you and your potential roommate stack up against each other. Put an *X* on the line where you fall, then an *O* on the line where your potential roommate falls. Look at the differences to see if these are things you can live with.

Qualities Spectrum

____*Organizational preferences:*

Everything has its place   **Likes the "cluttered look"**

____*Where cleaning is concerned:*

Cousin to the Tidy Bowl man   **Cousin to Peanuts character Pig Pen**

____*Morning person or night person:*

Believes early bird gets the worm   **"Who in the world wants a worm?"**

____*In relation to people:*

Always needs to be around them   **Needs to be alone most of the time**

____*Kind of room she likes best:*

Prefers the peace of the library   **Prefers the buzz of Grand Central Station**

____*In relation to God:*

Knows her Bible	Not likely to darken the church doors anytime soon

____*Her attitude toward money:*

Should be in Congress—likes a balanced budget	Thinks it grows on trees

The space in front of each quality/category is for you to prioritize the importance of this category to you. Next to the one that is most important to you, write a "1," for the second most important write a "2," and so on.

Now, go back over the list and see how you and your potential roommate compare on each quality, taking special note of those that you ranked as greater in importance to you.

Section 4
College Life

And So It Begins

ORIENTATION WEEK

Your first week on campus may give you a taste of what Columbus felt like when he stepped off the boat or what Neil Armstrong felt like when he planted his foot on the lunar surface. Your first week at college is a lot like being in a new world. To help you adjust to this newness, many colleges schedule an "orientation week." This orientation period usually takes place a few weeks before school officially starts. The upperclassmen have yet to arrive on campus, so the freshmen pretty much have the place to themselves. The school schedules a series of tours, seminars, question-and-answer sessions, and mixers to help students familiarize themselves with the campus, college life, and each other.

Orientation week can be a dizzying time. You may be intimidated by everything you need to learn and everyone you need to meet. Relax. Here are some tips that might help you as you prepare for orientation week.

EVERYBODY ELSE AT ORIENTATION FEELS THE SAME WAY YOU DO

You are not the only person at orientation worried about not fitting in at school. You're not the only one sweating the possibility of getting lost on campus. You're not the only one scared that you won't find anyone to talk to during the week. You're not the only one frightened of looking like a fool in front of the group.

Every freshman on campus is fretting about the same things, more or less. They're praying that someone—anyone—will talk to them. They're frantically writing down everything that's said, afraid that they're going to miss some vital piece of information. They're all worried about what's going to happen when the upperclassmen arrive on campus. Some of them may hide their fears better than others. Some of them may find refuge in groups. But every person in your freshman class is a bundle of insecurities.

DON'T WORRY ABOUT LEARNING EVERYTHING AT ONCE

You're going to be inundated with a boatload of instructions, directions, rules, regulations, and tips. In fact, you'll be presented with about ten times more information than you'll be able to retain. Don't worry about it. You've got plenty of time to learn—four years, in fact. You do not have to be a college expert by the time classes begin.

Start out with the basics. Memorize where you will live, where your classes will be, and where you will eat. Walk the route from your dorm room to each of your class sites—all the way to the classroom door, if possible—until you are confident that you know exactly where you're going. Then do the same for the dining hall. Once you've got your bearings straight, explore a little further. Locate the library, the gym, and any other place of interest to you on campus. Once you've got those locations down pat, branch out a little further. Acquainting yourself with the campus—particularly the places you'll need to be—will go a long way toward making you comfortable with college life.

Listen to Your Body

CATCH A CLUE

I'm not naturally a morning person, but when I scheduled my first semester of classes in college, I never gave that much thought. So I signed up for Old Testament Survey at 8:00 A.M. on Mondays, Wednesdays, and Fridays. I'll never forget the first class—my first college class ever! I'll also never forget the midterm exam or the final exam. I'll never remember the rest of those Old Testament classes that semester because I slept through every one of them. *Every one of them.* Fortunately for me, a friend of mine who was in the class with me taped all of the lectures. I ended up making a good grade in the course, but I had to sit through the lectures twice to do it—once in class and once on tape at night in the dorm. The next semester I signed up for New Testament Survey—at 2:00 P.M. —Suzanne, New York City

THINGS CHANGE

It's ironic that the most common affliction during orientation week is disorientation. But that affliction will soon pass. You'll be surprised at how quickly you adapt to the college setting and the college schedule. Do not be frightened away by the first week. Things change—quickly, and for the better.

The most important thing for you to remember is that orientation week is designed to help you, the freshman. If you have any questions at all, do not hesitate to ask. If you're having problems understanding anything at all, do not hesitate to get help. The people involved with freshmen orientation are paid to make you comfortable with school—both physically and emotionally.

Who, What, and When

SELECTING CLASSES

So many classes, so many professors, so many times of day—how in the world are you supposed to come up with a schedule that works for you? We've got a few ideas you might want to consider.

Consider your body's rhythm when you sign up for classes. If you're a morning person, load up your A.M. with class time and leave your afternoons free. If it takes you awhile to come alive, try to schedule only the most dynamic classes in the morning—the topics you're most interested in, the ones that will keep you awake.

One other consideration: If you're living in a dorm, you're not going to get as much sleep as you're used to. That's just the way it is. If you cram dozens of young, energetic students together in a small living area, peace and quiet are the first things to get chucked out the lounge window (followed closely by the couch cushions).

GET YOUR ADVISOR'S INPUT

Okay, let's just say this as nicely as we can. Sometimes your academic advisor may not be as helpful as you'd like. Now that's not a blanket statement by any means. There are many, many extremely helpful and knowledgeable advisors on college campuses around the country. For some faculty members, though, advising is a part of the job that they merely tolerate. They're unlikely to go out of their way to help you put together the best

schedule possible. Instead, most of them will look at the schedule *you've* already put together and say, "This looks good." If
they're feeling particularly helpful, they may look at their scheduling key and say, "You can't take News Reporting until you've
taken Intro to Journalism." They have a list of the core courses
you'll need for your degree, and they can advise you on those.
Beyond that, you're usually on your own. But don't sweat it.
Scheduling classes really isn't that hard to do.

LEARN FROM OTHERS' MISTAKES

"Dude, I had Edmonds for Biology, and he gave me hand
cramps with all the notes I had to take!"

"You've got to take Rousselow for Film Criticism. She went
to high school with George Lucas!"

You can't beat firsthand testimonials from upperclassmen.
If you want to know who's tough, who's funny, who's understanding, and who's a drill sergeant, talk to your fellow students,
people who have taken the classes before. You'll find that most
people don't need much prompting to start offering their opinions on a particular course or professor. Make sure, though, that
you talk to enough students to get the whole picture. Just
because one person thought a professor was tough doesn't
mean the professor was tough. Maybe the problem was with the
student.

Also remember that the things other people found intolerable
about a class or professor may appeal to you, and vice versa.
Maybe you're a great note taker and prefer a lecture-heavy course.
Maybe you thought *Star Wars* was overrated and have no desire to
sign up for a course taught by one of Lucas's high school classmates. Whatever the case, get as much advice as you can from
your fellow students, but take that advice with a grain of salt.

DO NOT EXCEED MAXIMUM WORKLOAD

Your course schedule is like a washing machine: It works best
with a balanced load. If you've talked to the professors, your
advisor, and students who have already taken those classes, you

have an idea of which classes will be a breeze and which ones are going to work your tail off. Try to schedule no more than one or two really tough classes each semester. Then even those classes out with one or two easier courses. As much as possible, try to prevent your schedule from being too difficult or too easy. Your goal is to achieve a harmonious balance between courses like Advanced Russian Literature and Intro to Basketball.

THINK IN CALENDAR TERMS

Make the calendar your friend when you schedule your semester courses. First, plan for your final exams. Most schools post an exam schedule in the registration office. Consult it so that you won't end up scheduling three classes with final exams on the same day.

Another trick that usually isn't mastered until sophomore or junior year is scheduling yourself a day off (or a light day). Load up on three Monday-Wednesday-Friday courses and two Tuesday-only classes, and what have you got? You've got yourself a day off! You can use Thursdays to run errands and study, with maybe a little goofing off thrown in for good measure. You'd be surprised what a day off in the middle of the week can do for your mental health.

TAKE WHAT YOU CAN GET

Here's where the rubber meets the road. You can do all the planning, investigating, reasoning, and interviewing you want, but when it comes down to doing the actual scheduling, you're at the mercy of the system.

The nasty fact is that freshmen are not allowed to register until after the seniors, juniors, and sophomores have registered for their classes. Which means that freshmen are left with the dregs after all of the other classes have filled up. That's life at the bottom of the food chain, right?

Maybe—and maybe not. If you try to schedule a class and are told that it's already full, you can either take the registrar's word for it and choose another class or you can check it out for yourself. Go talk to the professor of the class to plead your case.

You'd be surprised how often allowances are made to add a student to an already "full" class.

The Juggling Act

How to Balance School, a Job, and a Social Life

Balancing the three major aspects of college—class work, "work work," and a social life—is a lot like juggling. As you try to create a workable schedule that allows time for each of these elements, you'll feel like a performer trying to keep three balls in the air at the same time. That prospect may seem scary to you, until you discover the secret that almost all college students learn. With just a little practice, juggling isn't that hard to do.

Take Care of School First

First things first. Your whole reason for being at college is to get an education. (At least, that's what we'll assume for now.) Therefore, education becomes your first scheduling priority. If you're one who prefers to write down your schedule in an organizer or on a sheet of paper, start with your class periods. Block out the time each week that you will be sitting in lectures. Next, you'll need to think about study time. Some professors require their students to spend two hours studying *out* of class for every one hour they're *in* class. So for a three-hour biology course, you'll need to schedule six hours of homework. If you're taking a sixteen-hour load per semester, you're going to have to plan for thirty-two hours a week of homework.

This is important: The two-to-one ratio for homework hours to class hours is a rough average. Some professors require a three-to-one ratio. On the other hand, some courses require little or no outside work, so it evens out. You should be safe if you base your scheduling on a two-to-one ratio.

Depending on your high school study habits, you may have a little difficulty adjusting to collegiate class preparation. You'll find out (often the hard way) that seven two-hour study sessions a week are better than one fourteen-hour cramathon. With a little consistency and a lot of discipline, you'll learn how to do your studying in regular, bite-size chunks. You'll train yourself to do all that you need to do in each two-hour period. You'll also learn the importance of getting an early jump on writing term papers and studying for finals.

What's important to remember is that if you can get yourself into a routine in your studies, you're well on your way to balancing the other areas of college life.

EARN YOUR KEEP

We're going to assume for the moment that there are no trust-fund babies reading this section. We're going to assume that you're one of the millions of students who will be working one or more jobs at school for your tuition or spending money. If you are just such a person, you're in luck.

What we have for you is, hands-down, the all-time greatest piece of college-related advice in the history of the written word. Are you ready for this nugget of gold? Okay, here it comes:

Find a job, on campus or off, that allows you to study while you work. (That sound you heard was two birds being killed with one stone.) We've already seen that a sixteen-hour course load will require you to block out forty-eight hours on your weekly schedule (sixteen hours in class and thirty-two hours out of class). If you add fifteen hours of work a week to the schedule, suddenly you're booked for sixty-three hours a week! That's quite a load.

On the other hand, think about what happens when you find a job that allows you to study. You free up fifteen hours a week of your schedule. That's fifteen more hours for dating, playing sports, socializing, or sleeping!

You may be surprised at the number of jobs on campus that allow you to study while you work. Working the front desk at your dorm is one such job. Working in the library is another. Monitoring the gymnasium during intramurals is another. With a careful and thorough job search, you should be able to find a true "work-study" program.

DON'T NEGLECT YOUR SOCIAL LIFE

Okay, for some of you, that's like saying, "Don't forget to stare at a beautiful woman" or "Don't neglect to eat your lobster dinner." For some of you, your social life will be your number one priority in school. And while that's probably not a good idea, neither is underestimating the importance of that social life.

Real Education

There's more to college than classes. One high school **DON'T FORGET** teacher of mine used to say, "Never let your formal education get in the way of your real education." —Chris, North Haledon, NJ

Let's put it this way: You won't go back to your ten-year class reunion to visit your old accounting classroom or the dining hall where you washed breakfast dishes. You'll go back to see your friends, the acquaintances you made in school. Years from now, your social legacy will be most important to you. That's why it's vital that you schedule plenty of time for socializing, dating, and generally having a good time. The college years are among the best life has to offer. Don't ruin them with a schedule weighted too heavily toward academics and work. Live a little. No—live a lot!

Life Beyond the Classroom

CHOOSING EXTRACURRICULAR ACTIVITIES

All work and no play makes Jack a very frustrated college student. Sure, you've got to hit the books hard, but you've also got to experience life. Have fun. Explore your interests more fully. Make a difference in the world. The list of extracurricular activities you can pursue in college is much too long for us to include here. Instead, we offer some guidelines to help you in your decision making.

This is important: Before you start selecting your extracurricular activities, you need to make sure that you've accounted for your class work and any job you may have on your weekly schedule. Once those two areas are covered, you can use the time that's left for "fun stuff." (If you'd like more information on how to schedule various college responsibilities, read "The Juggling Act: How to Balance School, a Job, and a Social Life.")

TRY AN A LA CARTE APPROACH

Dabble in a little of everything—though not necessarily at the same time. Try something musical, like forming a band or learning to play an instrument. Try something artistic, like learning to draw or develop your own photographs. Try something political, like registering people to vote or putting up signs for a candidate. Your goal should be to leave college a well-rounded person, with hands-on experience in a wide variety of areas.

wow!

What I Learned in College

When I was a freshman, there was one guy on our floor who could juggle. By the end of the year, he had taught at least ten of us the skill. If you had walked into the floor lounge on any given evening, you'd have thought Ringling Brothers was holding an audition. You'd see ten guys juggling balls, rings, knives (yes, real knives), and anything else we could get our hands on. To this day, juggling is the only thing I can point to with certainty and say I learned in college.
—Jim, Hope, ID

GET OUT OF YOUR PIGEONHOLE

You're no longer constrained by your high school reputation. You can do whatever you want (within reason), without having to worry about what your friends will think. That's why we're suggesting that among your extracurricular activities you include one thing you've never done before. If you were a bookworm in high school, play an intramural sport. If you were shy and reserved, try out for a play. Don't dismiss an idea or a fleeting interest just because you can't picture yourself doing it.

FIND MENTORS AND TEACHERS WHERE YOU CAN

You'd probably be amazed at the talents and abilities of some of your fellow students, even the people who live around you. Take advantage of those abilities by asking those people to teach you what they know. This would be a good way to learn how to play the guitar, speak a foreign language, create killer web sites, and so on. Of course, if you have any talents, it would only be polite of you to volunteer to teach others what you know. Who knows? The whole thing could evolve into some talent-exchange program.

Do It As Much for the People As for the Activity

If a couple of your friends on campus are interested in an activity, give it a try with them, even if it doesn't sound interesting to you. Who knows, you may discover an interest you didn't know you had. Similarly, if there's an intriguing member of the opposite sex on the yearbook staff, volunteer for yearbook duty. Years from now you can tell your grandkids about how the two of you met in the yearbook photo lab. Activities are great, but it's the people that really matter. If you can be with your friends (or with someone you'd like to get to know), you can have a good time doing just about anything.

If You Don't Like It, Don't Do It

Yeah, you read that right. We're encouraging you to be a quitter. The college years are designed for experimenting and learning about one's self. So people will have to excuse a little flakiness and refusal to commit. College is too short and the life is too busy to spend time doing something you don't enjoy when you don't have to. You may hurt some feelings, and you may pick up a reputation as a flake, but that's okay. If you're convinced that something isn't for you, don't waste your precious time in college pursuing it.

This is important: The one exception to this rule is volunteer work. If you make a commitment to help a person in need or work on behalf of an organization that ministers to the needy, you must fulfill that commitment. Do not disappoint those people.

There's No Place Like Home

COPING WITH HOMESICKNESS

If you have any kind of relationship at all with your family, you're going to experience some homesickness when you leave for college. It's that simple. Come on, you've spent eighteen years with the people! Of course you're going to miss them! But homesickness does not have to mean misery. There are several things you can do to lessen the severity of your homesickness.

ADOPT A PIONEER ATTITUDE

Can you picture Christopher Columbus having a panic attack on the bow of his ship as he sailed for the New World? "What-a have-a I done-a?" he may have asked himself in a thick Italian accent. "I'm-a so far-a from-a my home-a. I miss-a my papa and-a my mama."

If the poor explorer had let these feelings grow, he may very well have turned his ships around and headed back to the Old World. But Chris didn't focus on what he left behind; he focused on the adventure and discovery that lay ahead.

That's exactly what you need to do. Think of yourself as an explorer. Focus on the adventure and newness that lies ahead rather than the safety and familiarity of what you've left behind. Report back to your family on the things you discover in the New World. Fill the heads of your younger siblings with exciting stories from abroad. Let them know the kinds of things they can expect when they set out on their own. Ask your family to send you a care package filled with goodies from home to make your journey more bearable.

WEAN YOURSELF FROM HOME SLOWLY

Don't try to go cold turkey in leaving your family. You'll never make it. If your parents can afford the phone bills, call home every night for the first week or so of school. Then cut back to three times a week, then to once a week. Talk for shorter and shorter amounts of time with each call until you've established a routine that works for both you and your family. As part of the weaning process, ask your family to send you a care package from home.

LET YOUR FAMILY KNOW HOW YOU FEEL

If you miss your parents and siblings so much, why not let them know? Be honest with them about how you're feeling. Tell them how much you appreciate them and what it is exactly that you miss about them. Thank them for all the support, encouragement, and love they've given you. Let them know how much you would appreciate a care package from home.

INVITE YOUR FAMILY TO YOUR NEW HOME

If your parents live relatively close to campus, extend an official invitation to them to visit your new home during Parents' Weekend. If you can, spend some time preparing for their visit. Think of the places you'd like to take them and the people you'd like them to meet. Give them a sense of what your new life is like. When they arrive, show them the time of their lives. Remind them that when visiting someone's new home, it's polite to bring a housewarming gift—say, in the form of a care package.

KEEP YOURSELF AS BUSY AS POSSIBLE

If you don't have time to think about what you're missing at home, it's likely you won't get homesick. Immerse yourself in college life. Focus on your classes and homework (although if "homework" makes you think of your family, you might want to call it "out of class work"). Spend time with your friends—or spend

CATCH A CLUE

Allow Yourself to Be "Adopted"

Many churches and college communities have adopt-a-student programs in which local families volunteer to provide support, encouragement, and weekly home-cooked meals for college students. Many young people find these programs to be the next best thing to spending time with their own families. What's more, having an adoptive family would in no way interfere with your receiving a care package from your real family.

time *making* friends. Check out the extracurricular activities your college has to offer. The quicker you get acquainted with everything your new home has to offer, the less you'll miss your old one. Before long, a simple care package from home will be all you need to stave off homesickness.

Four Years for Four Years: An Even Trade

THE ROTC PROGRAM ON CAMPUS

No matter how poor your family is, don't forget that you have a rich uncle who is ready, willing, and able to put you through college. Sound too good to be true? Allow us to introduce you to your Uncle. . .Sam.

That's right. In an effort to stock the United States' military with the finest young people available, the government will help finance a college education—with certain stipulations attached, of course. It's the government, after all. You can't expect something for nothing.

WHAT IT IS

The Army Reserve Officers' Training Corps (ROTC) is designed to train and qualify young men and women for appointment as second lieutenants in the United States Army, Army Reserve, or National Guard while they pursue their individual academic programs.

ROTC trains what the Army and civilian corporations are looking for—qualified leaders. Whether you are a physics major or a communications major, the skills you gain in Army ROTC will make you more marketable in the military or civilian world.

Should you decide to go the ROTC route, you will find yourself in some prestigious company. Among the men and women who have participated in the ROTC program are former president George Bush and General Colin Powell.

The Air Force and the Navy/Marine Corps offer similar

college programs: the Air Force Reserve Officers' Training Corps (AFROTC) and the Navy and Marine Reserve Officers' Training Corps (NROTC).

WHAT YOU'LL GET

Students who demonstrate excellence in academics, extra-curricular activities, and leadership may qualify for one of the scholarship programs offered by the ROTC (or the AFROTC or NROTC). Students may apply for nomination during their senior year of high school for a full four-year scholarship. Later in their college career, students may apply for shorter-term scholarships.

ROTC scholarships pay up to 80 percent of tuition per year, plus all required fees. Students also receive $450 yearly for books and supplies. AFROTC offers reimbursement for tuition and room and board, plus a monthly stipend to cover expenses. NROTC similarly pays for tuition and room and board but also covers books and fees, along with a monthly stipend.

WHAT YOU'LL STUDY

In addition to their course load, ROTC cadets study different levels of military science throughout their college stay. Military Science 101, which fresh-men may take during their first or second

CATCH A CLUE

Bonus Tip

Many corporations, especially those with veterans in executive positions, look favorably upon applicants with ROTC experience.

semester, is the introduction course designed to familiarize students with ROTC specifically and the Army in general. This course is worth three credit hours and is offered free of charge.

Military Science 201 is a lab course offered sophomore year. After taking this course, cadets may elect to contract into the advance program, complete their junior and senior courses, and receive a commission as a second lieutenant.

Juniors enroll in Military Science 301 and 302; seniors enroll in Military Science 401 and 402. As part of these courses, students may spend some weekends at actual Army bases, where they will practice the ROTC skills they have learned—from individual tactical training to running patrols. During these weekend maneuvers, cadets are evaluated on their leadership and teamwork skills.

What You'll Owe

In exchange for allowing the government to finance your education through ROTC, you agree after graduation to undergo six weeks of training with the Army, after which time you will receive a commission as a second lieutenant.

ROTC members may serve their four-year commitment in active duty in locations across the country and around the world or on a part-time basis in the U.S. Army Reserve or National Guard.

AFROTC graduates accept an Air Force Commission and serve actively for four years—five if flight training is involved. NROTC graduates accept a Navy or Marine commission for four years of active duty.

A four-year commitment after college is not something to be taken lightly. However, if you are simply looking for an inexpensive college education, ROTC (or AFROTC or NROTC) may be your best bet.

Call It an "Early" Graduation

When to Drop Out

Not all college careers end with a graduation. For some people, dropping out of school makes more sense than staying in. Not that it's an easy decision to make. Far from it. For one thing, there's the stigma that's attached to quitting. No one wants to be thought of as a "quitter." Then there's the matter of the green stuff (no, not the mold growing at the bottom of your dirty-clothes pile—we're talking about money). A semester of college costs *mucho dinero*. Dropping out and losing a semester, to some people, seems like a tremendous waste of money. That may be. But it's hard to argue against leaving school if that's what a person really *needs* to do. Here are some reasons as to why a person might need to drop out of school.

UNBEARABLE PRESSURE

Most people feel pressure when they go away to college. First, there's the weight of the academic expectations. The education process is much different in college than it is in high school. The lectures are more difficult to understand. The homework takes longer to complete. The tests are easier to fail. Learning is no longer the teacher's responsibility; it's the student's. For some people, the adjustments aren't that big of a deal. For others, they're like a whole new world.

Famous Dropouts

wow!

Even if you never finish college, that doesn't mean you're doomed to an unsuccessful and unfulfilled existence. Here are ten famous people who dropped out of college, all of whom seem to have done all right for themselves.

1. Garth Brooks
2. Matt Damon
3. Harrison Ford
4. Kathie Lee Gifford
5. Madonna
6. Gwyneth Paltrow
7. Robert Redford
8. Dennis Rodman
9. Steven Spielberg
10. Tiger Woods

Next there's the pressure of the social scene. For most people, starting college means starting over as far as friends are concerned. You've got to meet and get to know a whole new group of people in order to hang around with them. Some people get excited by that thought; others get depressed. Throw in the pressures of finding a job, getting along with a roommate, and sharing showers with dozens of other people, and you've got yourself a pressure cooker. If that pressure cooker is too much for you, you may need to consider dropping out of school.

FAMILY OR PERSONAL PROBLEMS

The prospect of staying in school in the midst of a family or personal crisis is almost unthinkable. Under the best of circumstances, college is tough. If you add a serious illness, a debilitating injury, a death in the family, or even extreme homesickness to the mix, it's nearly impossible. Unless you can focus completely on your academic responsibilities, you're in trouble. Therefore, if you experience an upheaval in your life during the school year, you may want to consider dropping out until the healing is complete.

MONEY CONCERNS

Unless you're absolutely certain that a degree is going to benefit you and your career later in life, college may be a tremendous waste of time and money for you. Consider the standard four years it takes to earn a bachelor's degree and the $80,000 or so it takes to pay for it (we're figuring an average of $20,000 per year for tuition and board). Carry those resources into another arena, and you've got some enviable capital for the venture of your choice. Think about those numbers. If you were to devote four years and $80,000 to a business of your own, imagine what you could do! For some people, this route is infinitely more practical than college. To them, a college education simply is not worth the price. The sooner they realize it and get out of college, the better off they'll be.

Dropping out of school is not an easy choice to make. It's also not a choice you should be ashamed of. Dropping out doesn't make you a loser. (Check out the list on the previous page for some famous college dropouts.) Dropping out doesn't mean you're stupid. In fact, if you drop out for the right reasons, you're probably wiser than the person who stays in school for the wrong reasons.

A Change of Heart

WHEN SHOULD YOU TRANSFER?

Here's the situation: You know you want to be in college; you're just not sure you want to be in college at the school you're attending. Maybe it's the academic program. Maybe it's the cultural opportunities. Maybe it's the social scene. Maybe it's the tuition. Maybe it's a combination of all four. The school may be fine for your fellow students, but for you, it just ain't happenin'. If that's the case in your situation, you might want to consider transferring to another school, my friend. Let's take a look at some of the situations that might justify a change of schools. Here are some circumstances that might lead you to consider transferring.

You're Bored

Not so fast, Slappy. Everyone's going to get bored occasionally (perhaps even three times a week in your Intro to Medieval Literature class). We're not talking about pulling out your suitcase any time there's nothing good on TV on a Friday night. That's not the kind of boredom that should lead to a change in academic institutions. We're talking about monotony of the soul, the boredom that results from not being challenged or engaged at your deepest level.

If you exist in a *constant* state of boredom on campus, if you're continually looking for something to interest you or hold your attention, it may be time to pull up stakes and head for greener pastures. If your present school is located in a rural area or small town, you may want to seek out the bright lights of the big city, perhaps an urban campus.

If, on the other hand, your boredom has academic roots, you may want to find a school that offers a more advanced program in your field of study. The last thing you want is to be bored by your own major.

Money Is a Problem

The cost of a college education is enormous. One day you may decide that you're paying too much for your education. (More likely your parents may decide that they're paying too much for your education.) Who's going to fault you if you want to save a couple "thou" here and there? Since chances are slim that you'll be able to negotiate a cheaper tuition rate for yourself at your present school (for some reason finance officers aren't open to dickering over the price), you may need to consider a less expensive option elsewhere.

You may also need to consider the fact that some schools may be offering better financial assistance packages. If you could lessen your debt load by $5,000 a year by attending a state school or (dare we even mention the possibility?) qualify for a scholarship at a smaller, less-known institute of learning, it may be worth your while to jump ship.

You Absolutely Need to Be Somewhere Else

One of the most irritating things about being human is our nagging tendency to make mistakes on occasion. Is it possible that you made a mistake when you chose your college?

The New Kid in Town

How to Adapt After Transferring

Being a transfer student can be tough. It's almost like being a beginning freshman, except that freshmen probably have it a little easier. As a transfer student, you still have to deal with all the problems that freshmen face—being new to the surrounding area, not knowing anyone, being unfamiliar with the campus layout—but you don't have the support group of other freshmen. You didn't go to orientation with hundreds of other people. You didn't have a chance to get to know anyone before school started. If you're a transfer student, you are truly the new kid in town. Throw in the added hassle of making sure your credits transfer and not losing ground in school, and you've got the potential for some trying times. Here are some things you'll need to remember if you decide to transfer.

Note: For the purpose of easy explanation, throughout this section we'll refer to your old school as "University A" and the school to which you're transferring as "University L." ("University B" would have been too obvious.)

Make Sure As Many Credits As Possible Transfer with You

Different universities have different academic requirements for graduation. What's more, individual universities determine which classes meet those requirements and which don't. For example, at University A, a course like Introduction to Classic Films may count toward your fine-arts requirement for graduation. Since you prefer watching movies to looking at sculptures and listening to classical music, you took the class to fulfill the requirement. After transferring, however, you find that University L does not recognize film as a fine-art and will not allow your credits from Intro to Classic Films to be applied to *its* fine-arts requirement, which basically means that you wasted your time in taking the film class at University A. Not only that, you're still faced with having to make up the fine-arts requirement at University L.

If enough credit hours fail to transfer like that, you may be staring at an extra semester in school. It's not terribly unusual for transfer students to go an extra semester, but it's not something you want to do if you can avoid it. We don't have to remind you that another semester in school means another several thousand dollars from your wallet (or your parents' savings account).

SPEND SOME TIME WITH THE PROFESSORS IN YOUR MAJOR

One of the first things you'll want to do when you get to your new campus is schedule some meetings with the people whose classes will mean the most to you. You're going to need to find out where you're at in comparison with the other students in your major. You may be advanced in some areas and lacking in others. Try to get a sense from the profs as to what you'll need to do in order to join your fellow majors in full stride.

If you find that University A was more advanced than University L is, especially in areas related to your major, you may discover that you have some expertise not enjoyed by your U of L classmates. If so, see if you can put that expertise to use for fun or profit. At the very least, you may be able to make a good impression on your future professors.

DON'T ACT LIKE A STRANGER IN A STRANGE LAND

It's important that you immerse yourself in school activities and campus life as quickly as possible. As far as making friends goes, perhaps the best place to start would be with the people in your major. For one thing, you'll automatically have something in common with them. For another, you'll be able to compare notes as to what you've learned so far—you at University A and they at University L.

Perhaps the best thing you can do for yourself is to erase the stigma of being a transfer student as quickly as possible. To do that, you'll need to be careful not to always bring up your old school or talk about how much better it was than University L. You'll also need to stop thinking of yourself as someone who dropped out of University A and start thinking of yourself as a student at University L!

To paraphrase the Beach Boys: Be true to your new school.

The Freshman Fifteen or Forty, Depending on Whom You Ask

DEALING WITH WEIGHT GAIN

Your mind and your horizons may not be the only things that expand when you get to college. Your waistline may do some flourishing as well. You've probably heard people talk about packing on poundage at college. But if you never had weight problems in high school, you're probably assuming you've got nothing to worry about—and you'll go right on assuming that until you find yourself wrestling with the top button of your jeans.

College weight gains have a way of sneaking up on you. Most people don't notice the extra girth until they're sporting a five- or ten-pound surplus. If the thought of such a weight gain has you breaking out in a cold sweat, here are some tips for you.

WATCH WHERE YOU GO FOR COMFORT

During your freshman year, you're going to be experiencing turmoil, uncertainty, and pressure unlike anything you've dealt with before. In the midst of such personal upheaval, you're probably going to look for comfort and reassurance wherever you can find it. Don't look for it in food.

Eating to relieve stress, to make yourself feel better, or to escape reality is the beginning of a dangerous progression that can lead to some serious disorders. Comfort comes from the Lord, from your family members, from your friends, and from yourself; comfort does not come from food. Any relief that food offers is temporary and illusory. Nothing about your situation changes when you eat.

GET YOUR REAR IN GEAR

Unless you're attending school on a planet whose oxygen level is incompatible with your body's needs, chances are you'll have plenty of opportunities for exercise every day at college. We're not talking about hitting the weight room or taking aerobics classes (though those aren't bad ideas, either). We're talking about quickening your pulse rate just by making small adjustments to your daily routine.

If you live in a high-

CATCH A CLUE

This Is Important

If you've had problems with eating disorders in the past, we strongly urge you to seek help as soon as you get to campus to avoid future problems. Do not underestimate the pressure you'll be under in college or overestimate your ability to handle it properly. Get help from a professional. There are plenty of support groups and counseling opportunities available on most campuses. Also, if you're comfortable with the idea, confide in your roommate or a trusted friend. Ask that person to watch you carefully for signs of eating disorders.

rise dorm, take the stairs instead of the elevator. Do not drive anywhere you can walk or ride your bike. During study breaks, go out for a stroll instead of stretching out in front of the tube. Take up a two-person sport with your roommate. It doesn't matter how good you both are, as long as you're fairly evenly matched. Even the most pathetic attempts at racquetball or tennis will give you a workout. And, of course, the more you play, the better you'll get. For more sporting fun, join an intramural

team—even if you're not naturally athletic. It's not about competition; it's about physical health.

MAKE JUNK FOOD AN INCONVENIENCE

Oh, the remorse of the overeater! "How could I have eaten that
entire bag of Oreos by myself?!" Well, you just reached over to the
conveniently placed package of goodies and grabbed a couple.
And then you did it again. And again. And again—until the only
evidence of cookies left were the telltale chocolate crumbs in the
corners of your mouth and the ink black junk between your teeth.

Here's a quick tip for you to keep in mind: If it's in your dorm
room, you're going to eat it. That being the case, why not stock
your room with things that are halfway decent, healthwise.
We're not suggesting that you go raid the rice-cake shelves of
your nearest grocery store. But you might want to keep some
fresh fruit in your refrigerator—or maybe some carrots or celery.
If you're just looking for something to munch on, there's no need
to blow your daily fat allowance on a bag of Chee•tos.
We're also not suggesting that you completely eliminate junk
food from your diet. Come on, it's college, after all! We're merely
suggesting that you banish it from your dorm room. Remember,
out of sight, out of mind (and out of belly).

Section 5
Making the Grade

In Study Mode

GET A GOOD STUDY LAMP

Your mother was right: you can't read in the dark. You certainly can't read effectively if you can't *see* what you're reading. Invest in a good study lamp or head to the library. Your eyes will thank you. (Even if you elect to study at the library, invest in a good study lamp. You may need to study in your dorm room someday. . . or you may need a light to investigate what's growing in your refrigerator.)

LOOK FOR A QUIET PLACE

You will need a quiet place in order to concentrate. A library carrel may be your home away from home for the next four years. Or, perhaps when your roommate leaves, the noise level in your dorm room quiets down a decibel or two. Decide where you study best. Wherever you decide is the ideal study place, consider the possible distrac-

THE BIBLE SAYS

Be Diligent

"Be diligent to present yourself approved to God, a worker who does not need to be ashamed, rightly dividing the word of truth." (2 Timothy 2:15 NKJV)

A person who studies is a worker who will not be ashamed when called upon to stand the test—namely, a midterm or final!

tions you may face. If you're easily distracted, you may need to invest in earplugs or earphones and instrumental CDs.

READ WHAT THE PROF ASSIGNS

If your professor says to read pages 83–184, that's what he or she expects you to read. Doing the assigned reading is *effective reading* in a nutshell. Even if you find the reading to be pointless, try to do it anyway. There's usually a method to the madness.

LEARN TO SKIM READ

If you've been assigned ten books for *each class* you're taking this semester and you're in a time crunch (what student isn't?), learn to skim read. Skim reading saves time. (If you *do* have the time, however, do *all* of the assigned reading.) When you skim read, you need to understand the main idea and supporting details of a paragraph. The main idea is usually described

To Read or Not to Read

Effective reading can mean the difference between whether you pass a test or not. If

CATCH A CLUE

you don't understand the directions—or worse, don't follow them—your reading has not been effective. (For more on exams, read "It's *What* You Know That Counts" and "The Final Frontier.")

in the topic sentence. The details that follow build on or support that idea. There may be some ideas you can skip and still understand what the paragraph was all about.

Before you skim read, you'll need to look through the reading first to gauge what to read fully and what you can safely skim. This is the *S* of SQ3R. (See "Use the SQ3R Method.")

HIGHLIGHT IMPORTANT SENTENCES AND SECTIONS

Keep a supply of highlighters handy. Since you won't be able to retain every single word you read (not even with *CliffsNotes*), highlighting *highlights* key points to remember. Highlight important concepts and definitions, main ideas, and points that express good arguments or opinions that resonate with you. The points that are easiest to remember are the ones that strike a chord within you. These points may come in handy during an essay test or when you want to bring up a point in class.

When you need to study for midterms and finals, those highlighted portions can cue you to important content. (For more on exams, see "It's What You Know That Counts.")

USE THE SQ3R METHOD

SQ3R or $SQR^1R^2R^3$ is actually a formula. "SQRRR?" you say. "Sounds like a rusty gate opening!" Yet, this little ditty, developed by Francis P. Robinson, can help you improve your studying. The letters stand for Survey (S), Question (Q), Read (R^1), Recite (R^2), Review (R^3). (See Francis P. Robinson, *Effective Study* (New York: Harper and Row, 1970.) The formula must be used in the order given.

Survey (S). Focus on what you are reading. In other words, "pay attention and gain understanding" (Proverbs 4:1). This may include previewing the material to be read and deciding how long the reading will take. Flip through the book and skim the content. Check the table of contents. Look at the visual aids. Read the chapter titles and subheads.

Question (Q). After you survey, you'll probably have questions. Asking questions about the reading can help you develop a

Homework

wow!

You've got your favorite CD blasting. Microwave popcorn's in reach. The TV is switched to a show you've seen before. Now you're ready. *For what?* you say. To study of course. . .or not.

In high school, a study period was built into your schedule as a reminder to study. At home your parents were on hand to nag you into studying (if you required that). In college, you cannot count on anyone—not your prof, not your roommate, not your best friend—to *make* you study. You are an adult. It's up to you to make the grade. This takes wisdom. (See Proverbs 13:10; 23:23.)

The key to studying is to read effectively. Effective reading means you understand and can retain at least some of what you've read. So. . .how can you read effectively?

purpose for doing the reading. What do I know about this topic? What did the prof assign me to read? What questions do the titles and subheads suggest?

Read (R^1). Although you might think that this should be the first step (RSQRR anyone?), it's actually the third. Reading can help answer the questions you developed while surveying.

Recite (R^2). Go over what you read either by reciting the material orally or through note taking. You don't have to do this after every paragraph, however. You can decide for yourself when you need to stop and recite.

Review (R³). This step involves the whole SQ3R method. Survey once more to see what you remember, check whether your questions have been answered, reread your notes, then recite what you know.

IMPROVE YOUR VOCABULARY

Read any book on studying ("read a book on studying?!!" you say) and you'll find they all say the same thing: Improving your vocabulary can help you read more effectively. "Why?" you ask. Good question. The truth is, vocabulary skills can help you better identify concepts and the contexts in which they are used. Once you understand the *denotation* (dictionary definition) and *connotation* (implied meaning) of a concept and its context, you can retain the information, rather than drown in hopeless *obfuscation.* (Dictionary, anyone?) So, keep a dictionary nearby in case you need to look up a word.

TAKE BREAKS

Reading can be tiring on the eyes. To avoid eyestrain, take study breaks to refresh your eyes. (An eight-hour study break does not count.)

FIGHT PROCRASTINATION

You might be a procrastinator. . .if your motto is one of the following:

> "Why put off till tomorrow what you can put off till next week?"

> "If you wait until the last minute, it only takes a minute to do."

> "The sooner you get behind, the more time you have to catch up."

Waiting until the last minute is a universal habit. It is also one that you will need to break to avoid an all-nighter. An all-nighter is an all-night cram session. An all-nighter won't solve all of your problems, however. If you keep on top of what you need to study, you won't feel as frantic about whether you've read effectively. (See "The Paper Trail" and "The Final Frontier" for more on all-nighters.)

Keep a Journal of Your Assignments

Gary Bergreen, in his book *Coping with Study Strategies* (New York: The Rosen Publishing Group, 1986), suggests that keeping an assignment journal is a good thing. You might keep track of your assignments and how effectively you've read the material. A journal might also help you budget your study time wisely (and avoid *some* stress).

Internet Study Tools

For Starters

If you want to combine studying and computers, get ready to surf the Net. These sites can help get you started.

- www.gospelcom.net (a resource for Christian organizations, colleges, and so on)
- www.insight.org (Insight for Living's site; if you like Chuck Swindoll and need to take a devotional breather, head for this site to hear each day's program)
- www.altavista.digital.com (Alta Vista can help you find other sites)
- www.collegeboard.org
- www.yahoo.com (you'll say, "Yahoo!" when you've made a successful search through Yahoo)
- www.aol.com
- www.cliffs.com (the Cliffs Notes site)
- www.cnn.com (the CNN site provides news)
- www.loc.gov (the site of the Library of Congress)
- www.usnews.com (the site of the magazine *U.S. News and World Report*)

- www.newsweek.com (*Newsweek's* site)
- www.time.com (three guesses as to which magazine has this site)

SUBJECT RESEARCH

The Internet is a great tool for research. Although it is not meant to be your *only* source of information, it can *help* you find *added* information in your subject. For instance:

Resources

DON'T FORGET

Netstudy by Wolff New Media LLC [Michael Wolff] (New York: Dell, 1997) is the book to buy or at least borrow from the library. It lists thousands of educational sites on the Web. The book is divided by subject (English, Mathematics, Chemistry, and so on) with web sites for all. Run—don't walk—to the nearest campus bookstore or library to find this book.

The research librarian at your college library can also help you find what you need on the Internet. He or she may provide more assistance with search databases.

English Literature

There are several web sites for well-known authors. Some include excerpts from their most popular works.

- Jane Austen—uts.cc.utexas.edu/~churchh/janeinfo.html
- Samuel Coleridge— www.lib.virginia.edu/etext/stc/Coleridge/stc.html
- Ralph Ellison—www.english.upenn.edu/~afilreis/50s/ellison-main.html
- Ernest Hemingway—www.ee.mcgill.ca/~nverever/hem/pin-dex.html
- Herman Melville—www.melville.org
- William Shakespeare—the-tech.mit.edu/Shakespeare/works.html
- Mark Twain—web.syr.edu/~fjzwick/twainwww.html

There are copies of some books on-line. Find a book like

Netstudy that lists books on-line. You might also do a title search at one of the sites under "For Starters."

Math
If you need help with a problem, consult your prof or TA. You might also ask him or her to recommend some good math sites you can access. Here are a few in the math vein.

- For basic math, check out CTC Math/Science Gateway— Mathematics www.tc.cornell.edu/MathSciGateway/math.html
- For calculus—www.math.ohio-state/~davis/cmremote.html
- For on-line math help—forum.swarthmore.edu/dr.math/ dr-math.html (the Ask Dr. Math! site; sponsored by Swarthmore College)

Biology
From African primates to zoology, the Web has sites for you.

- The CTC Math/Science Gateway: Biology— www.tc.cornell.edu/MathSciGateway/biology.html
- On Compuserve—*go* science®Libraries *or* Messages®biology
- www.exploratorium.edu/learning_studio/cow_eye (if dissecting cow eyes is your idea of fun, this is the site for you)

Chemistry
To ponder polymers, check out these sites:

- odin.chemistry.uakron.edu/analytical/
- the-tech.mit.edu/~davhsu/chemicool.html (a site devoted to the periodic table)
- www.cetlink.net/~yinon/index.html (another site devoted to the periodic table)

Physics
Intrigued with inertia? If you're not fully inert, check out:

- www-pdg.lbl.gov/cpep.html
- www.physics.mcgill.ca/deptdocs/physics_services.html
- www.eia.doe.gov/energy (the Department of Energy's site)

Anthropology
If Indiana Jones really revved you up to study anthropology, these sites may also get your motor going:

- www.acs.oakland.edu/~dow/anthap.html (The Applied Anthropology Computer Network)
- www.lawrence.educ./dept./anthropology/classics.html (where you can go for your anthropological needs)

Economics
Whether macro or micro, money matters are on-line:

- econwpa.wustl.edu/EconFAQ/EconFAQ.html
- www.money.com (*Money* magazine's site)

Ethnic Studies (African-American, Asian, Hispanic, Native American Studies)

- www.afroam.org
- www.amagazine.com
- www.iprnet.org/IPR
- www.afn.org/~native

Women's Studies
Many sites are sponsored by NOW (the National Organizaton for Women) or linked to NOW's web site.

- www.getnet.com/women.html
- www.now.org/now/home.html

Psychology
For some of your psychological needs, these sites may prove helpful:

- www.apa.org (sponsored by the American Psychological Association)
- www.indiana.edu/~iuepsyc/P103Psyc.html
- www.gasou.edu/psychweb/selfquiz/selfquiz.htm
- www.exploratorium.edu/learning_studio/lsxhibit.html

History

You can find information on all types of history on the Internet.

- www.sas.ac.uk/School/Historical.htm
- miavx1.acs.muohio.edu/~ArchivesList/index.html (New Orleans Archives site)
- sunsite.unc.edu/expo/deadsea.scrolls.exhibit/iintro.html (three guesses what this site is all about just by looking at the name)
- rs6.loc.gov/amhome.html (the Library of Congress's American Memory site features essays on American history)

Foreign Languages

French, Spanish, German, Japanese—there is a site for you.

- humanities/uchicago.edu/forms_unrest/FR-ENG.html (French-to-English dictionary)
- www.itc.omron.com/cgi-bin/j-e (Japanese-to-English dictionary)

Geared Up for Graduation

"There is a time for everything, and a season for every activity under heaven," as Ecclesiastes 3:1 says. The season of college life has traditionally been four years. Now many major programs make the five-year plan a

THE BOTTOM LINE

Be Diligent

"We want each of you to show this same diligence to the very end, in order to make your hope sure." (Hebrews 6:11)

necessity. Graduating from college "on time" *is* possible. After all, many people have done so. It takes good scheduling, careful attention to detail, persistence, and a lot of prayer.

FULFILL YOUR DISTRIBUTION REQUIREMENTS

Remember those distribution requirements (*general education requirements*) as discussed in "Choosing a Major"? You *cannot* complete your degree without fulfilling all requirements or placing out of them. See your college catalog for more details, or call the registrar's office. If you know you have to take a foreign language or a math course and need help, seek tutoring early. Or, take the class in summer school. *Do not* sign up for a summer school course without first checking whether the credit will be accepted.

Declare a Feasible Major

Your college has rules for when and how to declare a major. (See also "Choosing a Major.") If you want to change your major and still complete your degree within four years, make sure you decide early on. Some major switches have a time penalty that you cannot overcome. For example, switching from biochemistry to English literature in your junior year may keep you from graduating within four years because of the prerequisites you have to make up.

To Each His Own

There was a senior I knew when I was a freshman at NU. He was supposedly a senior then. But when I was a senior, he was still a se-nior! I wondered, *Does he just like the school? Are his parents wealthy? Is he on the eight-year plan?* I later saw him on TV as a regular on *Saturday Night Live.* I guess his eight-year plan didn't really damage his career.
—Bob, Chicago, IL

Complete Sequence Courses

Each sequence course is a prerequisite for another in the sequence. You can't move on until you pass each course. The beginning of the sequence is usually offered once a year. If you don't pass this class, you'll have to wait until the following year. This is especially important for sequence courses that are pre-requisites *for the following year's* sequence courses.

Carry a Full Course Load Each Semester or Quarter

Some schools require three to four classes per quarter or four to five per semester as a full-time student. If you have to drop a class one quarter or semester, be prepared to take an extra class during the following quarter/semester if necessary.

Determine how many courses are required for the comple-tion of the degree program. For example, Northwestern

University (Evanston, Illinois) requires 45 course credits for graduation. On a three-quarter system (fall, winter, and spring), a student would have 48 course credits if he or she took four courses each quarter—more than enough to graduate. This allows some leeway if you have to drop a class one quarter or if heavy course work demands that you take three classes, rather than four. Keep track of the credits or credit hours you have and how many more you'll need in order to graduate.

The Proof Is in the Professor

PROFESSORS ARE EXPERTS IN THEIR FIELD

The old adage "those who can't, teach" isn't true for college professors. There are all different types of professors. Some are Nobel-prize winners. Others are nationally known for their field of study.

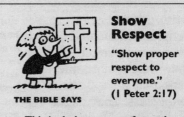

Show Respect

"Show proper respect to everyone." (1 Peter 2:17)

THE BIBLE SAYS

This includes your professors!

Some are a dream to listen to, others are more challenging. Some professors invite dialogue from students. Some prefer the "I'll do the lecture" approach. Some allow their TAs (teaching assistants) to lecture.

Being an expert means having opinions. There are some points a professor may make that you'll agree with and some that may offend or enrage you. If there is a point to which you disagree, you could make an appointment to talk to the professor or ask questions during Q & A. Few professors like to be confronted in class by how much a student *thinks* they don't know. During your time at college, you may be in a class where a student is confrontational in an effort to show how smart he or she is. Some professors are better able to handle this than others; some might even welcome argument. Yet even if you feel you know more than the professor or TA, there is one undeniable fact about him or her—he or she has *already* received the degree to which you're trying for, *plus* others. Hebrews 13:17

reminds us to obey our leaders and "submit to their authority." This is not always easy, but it is possible.

Which brings up another point. If you're trying to toady up to a popular professor, here's a word to the wise: don't. There is nothing wrong with wanting to know a professor. But be sincere. No one likes a yes-person.

PROFESSORS ARE HUMAN

They have good and bad days just like you do. In addition to teaching class, they also have projects of their own to work on or books to write. Since they're people, that means they're not perfect. They may forget your name, especially if you're in a large class. They might assign truck loads of work and actually expect you to do it. They might even make a mistake now and then. If you feel that a

THE BOTTOM LINE

Who's the Prof?

What's that blur that just ran past you? Why it's your professor racing away from class to get safely behind the closed door of his or her office. This is the image that many students have of their profs: a person who lectures, then streaks away to an office that he or she is never seen in. While not always the case, some profs are more challenging than others to get to know. Can they be known? Is it even *possible* to get that prize many students covet—an appointment with them during their office hours? You can know the answers to these questions as you examine what makes up this breed of animal known as the college professor.

professor or TA has made a mistake in your grade (and you have reasonable evidence to back this up), make an appointment to talk as soon as you can. Be persistent until you can get in to see him or her. Don't assume that he or she will automatically know what you need.

The Paper Trail

TERM-PAPER TEST

The dreaded moment has arrived: You have to write a paper.
Do you:

A. Blow it off until the night before it's due?
B. Get started on it before the professor has even thought to assign it?
C. Ask the Lord to rapture the church before the paper is due?
D. None of the above?
E. All of the above?

It's safe to assume that you will have to write a paper of some type before you leave college. Whatever your style of handling it, the fact is, it has to be done! Let's say your prof hands

Good Advice

"Fix these words of mine in your hearts and minds....Write them [down]...."

DON'T FORGET (Deuteronomy 11:18–20)

you a topic: Write a critical essay on the TV sitcom and its relationship to the couch potato's view of life, gnosticism, and wealth. So, what do you do? The steps of the writing process (yes, what you learned in fifth grade and back in high school) still hold true.

PREWRITING

In this stage, think about what you already know about the topic. Ask yourself questions based on what you would need to cover in your paper. If you're the type that thrives on order, you might list each question on an index card along with a primary or secondary source you can go to for information. Will you use interviews of couch potatoes? firsthand accounts? notes from class? Once you decide on the research you need, pray. Ask God to help you have a productive time as you research. Then hit the libes! The search databases libraries use will enable you to find sources there, plus periodical information.

You might do some of your research on-line. Yahoo (www.yahoo.com) and Alta Vista (www.altavista.digital. com) can help you go where you need to go. (See "Internet Study Tools" for other search options.)

If your prof placed books on reserve in the library for class research use, the books are meant to be used there. Unfortunately, some students determine that material on reserve gives them license to rip out pages they need or (heaven forbid) steal them. If the material you need isn't there, alert the library staff and the prof.

Once you've done your research, it's time to write. . .the outline. For an essay, an outline is. . .well. . .critical. An outline helps you organize the structure of your paper from the introduction to the conclusion.

DRAFTING

The first thing to think about when drafting a paper for college is this: You're not in high school anymore, Toto. Your prof expects you to develop your thoughts into a well-reasoned argument with an appropriate conclusion. With that in mind, avoid starting out by repeating the topic word for word within the topic sentence of your introduction. Professors (or TAs) know

Computer Rule #1

CATCH A CLUE

If you've typed your paper on a computer, make sure you save your work frequently. There have been many who toiled for hours without saving their work, only to have their computers suddenly freeze. They were forced to reboot, which meant they lost all of their work. It *could* happen to you! Make a backup copy of your paper when you finish.

when you're stalling: "My topic—the TV sitcom and its relationship to the couch potato's view of life, gnosticism, and wealth—is a very intriguing one." Get to the point. The questions you developed in prewriting will help you nail your introduction. Don't worry about getting it just right the first time out, however. Just write for now. Your first draft does not have to be perfect.

If you use footnotes, be sure to include a "Works Cited" page or bibliography. One important tip to consider: Do not invent sources! Use authentic source material.

REVISING

Now you're ready to perfect your paper (or get it as close to perfection as a human creation can get). Weed out those wordy passages you hastily jotted down during the first draft. Double-check your footnotes and references for accuracy. Make sure your conclusion rounds out the thoughts expressed in your introduction.

When you need help with style issues, use *The Chicago Manual of Style* (current edition), by the University of Chicago Press; *A Manual for Writers*, by Kate L. Turabian; or *Elements of Style*, by Strunk and White. These are time-honored sources. Also look for *Punctuate It Right!* by Harry Shaw (New York: Harper Collins, 1993 or more recent edition) and *Essentials of English* by Vincent F. Hopper, Cedric Gale, Ronald C. Foote, and Benjamin W. Griffith (Hauppage, New York: Barron's Educational Series, Inc., 1990 or more recent edition).

EDITING/PROOFREADING

This is the time to check your grammar, punctuation, and check for typos. Don't forget to spell check the file. You'll have to catch your own homonym mistakes, however. The computer won't know if you really meant *read* but typed *red*. Some word-processing programs have a grammar check you can employ. You may have to be selective about the advice you take. (Many grammar checks are keen on passive voice "mistakes.") Now print out a copy of your paper and read it through. Don't proofread it on the screen. Some typos have a way of hiding from the eye while a document is on the screen. Typos and other inaccuracies can lower your grade, even if your paper is well written.

You might read the paper out loud or read parts of it to your roommate. Reading something out loud can help you understand whether the expressed thoughts are cohesive.

FINISHED PAPER

You're ready to hand in that paper. Should you slip it into an acetate binder or something fancier? Will the "tried-and-true" staple method suffice? When in doubt, ask your professor or TA.

A Word About Plagiarism

Don't. Plagiarizing—copying another writer's work and calling it your own—can cost you. Many students have failed a class or been expelled from universities for plagiarism. While this might not seem like the crime of the century, it *is* a strike against your trustworthiness. Hebrews 13:18 says, "We are sure that we have a clear conscience and desire to live honorably in every way." You're on the honor system when you write a paper. That

Plagiarism Isn't a Good Idea

My fraternity had archives of old term papers. These were **wow!** *technically* only for reference use, but one late night temptation got the better of me. I took a term paper and retyped it as my own. I turned it in with my name on it. A couple weeks later I received it back in class with the following note from the professor: "This was an 'A' paper—when I wrote it 20 years ago. Please see me after class." —Josh, 19

means your prof is expecting you to use your own words. You *are* allowed to quote part of an author's work, however. Whenever you do, you must cite the source.

If You Have to Pull an All-Nighter

Don't. But you probably will anyway, if you like to procrastinate. Since God designed the human body to require sleep, you may be tempted to use artificial means in order to stay awake: coffee, soda, tea. These items, in abundance, will make you jittery. Take a cold shower if necessary. The best advice about all-nighters is to avoid taking pills of any kind and at least get *some* sleep. When your body craves sleep, you cannot get your best work done.

If You Have to Rewrite a Paper You've Turned In

The professor will let you know what needs to be done and will give you a time frame in which to do it. If you need help, make an appointment with him or her to talk about your paper. If you're feeling absolutely overwhelmed about writing the paper in general, check with the professor or fellow students for information on where you can go to find assistance.

It's What You Know That Counts

ME? TAKE EXAMS?

How hard are exams? Very—if you're not prepared. Unless you have an IQ of 200 and don't have to study, studying is to your best advantage. Attending class and taking notes are also ways you can be prepared for tests.

Midterms and finals are stopping points to determine how you're doing in a class. The prof usually explains what percentage each test counts

God Can Help

THE BIBLE SAYS

"Now to Him who is able to do immeasurably more than all we ask or imagine, according to His power that is at work within us, to Him be glory in the church and in Christ Jesus throughout all generations, for ever and ever! Amen." (Ephesians 3:20–21)

If you panic at just the thought of a test, consider how God can help. But don't use prayer as an excuse not to study!

toward your grade. For example, midterm = 25%; papers = 25%; final = 50%. If you do poorly on your midterm exam, you might be able to pull up your grade on the final, or through other assignments. If you know your midterm exam counts for a low percentage, do your best anyway. Do not use this as an excuse to slack off.

THE BIG BLUE-BOOK WORLD

Essays

Before you finish college, you may come to dread the sight of blue. Blue books—those little blue booklets with lined pages—are given out for answers to essay questions and short-answer questions. Some essay tests might consist of one question to synthesize what you've read or discussed in the class. Be sure to read the directions or pay attention if the question is given orally.

Many profs dislike having you repeat the question as part of your answer. To start off with something like "The question, 'Are dolphins really capable of speech?' is a good question and one that is pertinent for discussion" may net you some points off. Profs know a stall technique when they see it. (See also "The Paper Trail.") Since you have a limited amount of time in which to work, your time will best be served by answering the question.

Problems
You'll find exams with problems to solve in math and science classes. Treat these exams as you did the SAT or ACT. If you don't know an answer, skip it until you can come back to it later. You're working against time. When in doubt, take your best guess. There may be a penalty for wrong guesses, however.

Take-Home Tests
Many students love the take-home test, because class notes or the assigned texts can be used (if the prof has given his/her OK). Take-home tests are sometimes harder than in-class tests because of their open-book nature. If you did not attend class all semester or read the assigned texts, you will have a difficult time even with a take-home test.

STRATEGIES
The best test-taking strategy there is is to be prepared for it.

Get Some Sleep the Night Before
A prepared mind is a well-rested one. If you can, avoid all-nighters. (See the section on all-nighters in "The Paper Trail.") If you find you need to stay up, drink caffeinated soda or coffee, but be prepared to be jittery. Avoid studying on your bed, or you will fall asleep. Keep in mind also that one hazard of an all-nighter is that you could wind up falling asleep during the test. You don't want that!

Read the Directions and Questions Carefully
You might feel tempted to skim a question just to save time. Do yourself a favor: Read the whole question to make sure you *know* what's expected.

Keep Track of Time

Keeping track helps you pace yourself. If the exam is an hour and a half and you have 35 questions, you don't want to waste 45 minutes trying to figure out one you don't know.

Read Over Your Answer

In your haste to write, you might skip writing an important word or miscalculate. If you have the time, check your work.

The Final Frontier

THE END IS NEAR

Finals week is coming. Will you be prepared? You can be.

CHECK WITH YOUR PROFS

Each prof will let you know what material will be covered on the final and how much the final counts toward your grade. Some may even let you work toward doing your best by showing you an old exam or holding a review session. Take advantage of any resources you're given.

THE BIBLE SAYS

Tests

"Dear friends, don't be surprised at the fiery trials [tests] you are going through, as if something strange were happening to you." (1 Peter 4:12 NLT)

Facing an exam can feel like a fiery trial. While you may not feel as "glad" as the apostle Peter suggests in verse 13, you *can* be glad about one thing: You *can* get help to pass the test!

STAGGER YOUR STUDYING

Your finals are usually staggered, based on when each class is scheduled. You'll want to study for each class in the order in which the final will take place. So don't get caught up in studying for next Friday's Spanish final if your calculus final is this Monday.

Decide Where and How You Study Best

A library carrel might be the place for you. Most college libraries are open late, particularly during finals week. The only disadvantage is having to get up and go there and track down a good spot. Many students opt for studying in their dorm rooms to avoid the crowd at the library. Studying in your dorm room or frat house might be difficult, especially if you have a roommate or neighbors trooping in and out. If you have a room to yourself, great. But keep in mind the distractions your room might offer: the phone, your bed, loud neighbors.

Some university libraries have unofficial "breaks" at certain times. For many years at Northwestern University, the "nine-o'clock break" was an understood social time at the vending machines. If you're distracted by this (particularly if several of your friends are hanging out at the library that night), you may want to have a place to escape to continue your studying in peace.

Finals Week Munchies

DON'T FORGET

Many dorms provide munchies for students during finals week. Your RA will let you know when, where, and what snacks will be served. This is important information that *will not* be on the final.

Some students have found study groups helpful. Try to find one that is right for you. If you study best alone, don't feel obligated to seek a group.

Avoid Too Much Caffeine

If you're forced to pull an all-nighter to study for the exam, don't submerge yourself in caffeine. Caffeine eventually works against your concentration. Sleep is your best option.

Don't Panic

If you've made it to class all semester or quarter and studied for the exam, you should pass the final. If you know you're not a good test taker, don't let finals jitters get you in a panic or make you feel as if you'll forget everything you know. Instead, pray. But don't expect prayer to take the place of your studying for the test. God can help you recall what you already know; He will *not* supply information you never read.

Do Your Best

If you know you've studied as hard as you could, pull yourself out of worry mode and make up your mind to do your best. Keep in mind that some courses are unofficially designed to weed out a certain amount of students. Therefore, the final might be very difficult. At one university three-fourths of the students in the first-level chemistry class failed the final. While this may seem unfair, it *is* a fact of college life. You're *still* obligated to do your best regardless of whether or not your program is designed to weed out freshmen.

A Word About Cheating

Don't.

wow!

How (Not) to Write a Term Paper

(This list was circulated around the Internet. Our thanks to the unknown author.)

1. Sit in a straight, comfortable chair in a clean, well-lighted place with plenty of freshly sharpened pencils.
2. Read over the assignment carefully, to make certain you understand it.
3. Walk down to the vending machines and buy coffee to help you concentrate.
4. Stop off at another floor on the way back and visit with your friend from class. If your friend hasn't started the paper yet either, you can both walk to McDonald's and buy a hamburger to help you concentrate.
5. When you get back to your room, sit in a straight, comfortable chair in a clean, well-lighted place with plenty of freshly sharpened pencils.
6. Read over the assignment again to make absolutely certain you understand it.
7. You know, you haven't written to that kid you met at camp since fourth grade. You'd better write that letter now; that way you can concentrate.
8. Go look at your teeth in the mirror.
9. Listen to one side of your favorite tape and that's it, I really mean it, as soon as it's over you are going to start that. . .
10. Listen to the other side.
11. Rearrange all of your CDs.
12. Phone your friend on the other floor and ask if he's started writing yet. Exchange derogatory remarks about your teacher, the course, the university, and the world at large.
13. Sit in a straight, comfortable chair in a clean, well-lighted place with plenty of freshly sharpened pencils.
14. Read over the assignment again; roll the words across your tongue; savor its special flavor.
15. Check the *TV Guide* to make sure you aren't missing something truly worthwhile on TV (like football).
16. Go look at your tongue in the mirror.
17. Sit down and do some serious thinking about your future.
18. Open your door and check to see if there are any mysterious, trench-coated strangers lurking in the hall.
19. Sit in a straight, comfortable chair in a clean, well-lighted place with plenty of freshly sharpened pencils.
20. Read over the assignment one more time, just for the heck of it.
21. Scoot your chair across the room to the window and watch the sunrise.
22. Lie facedown on the floor and moan.
23. Leap up and write the paper.
24. Type the paper in your computer.
25. Spell check.
26. Complain to everyone that you didn't get any sleep because you had to write that stupid term paper.

Section 6
The Money Pit

Balancing and Budgeting

IMAGINE. . .

Imagine if your car had no gas gauge. You put in gas and drive, never knowing for sure how much gas you have left. Then, one day, on the way to an important appointment, the car suddenly dies. As you coast to the side of the road (if you're lucky), you realize that, once again, you're out of gas. Some people look at their checkbooks that way. Toss in some money, write some checks, draw some money from the ATM, use the debit card a few times, all the while thinking they have the balance "in their heads." Then, when they *really* need a few dollars, the ATM won't give it because they recently wrote a check that overdrew their account. Add to that overdraft charges and. . .well, you get the picture. Just as you constantly look at the gas gauge in your car, so you *must* keep track of the balance in your checkbook.

WHY BOTHER? I HAVE ENOUGH TO DO!

Balancing your checkbook is important and need only take a few minutes each month. That few minutes can save you a lot of Excedrin! But the only way to balance a checkbook is to first keep track of *every* transaction you make during the month. That means *every* check, deposit, ATM withdrawal, debit-card transaction. That's what that other little packet in your checkbook is for—you know, the one with the lines and the columns. It's called the check "register." No, not what you did in order to get into college, but what you need to keep track of in order to have enough money to *stay* in college.

It may help you to get what are called duplicate checks—these have a carbonless copy of each check. But you still need to keep a running record of *all* transactions. You must train yourself to write everything in the check register so that you will always know your "balance"—not how well you stand up but how well you stand regarding how much money you have. This will keep you from "overdrafts"—not the cold breeze that blows into your dorm room but bounced checks. Your bank has a rather "cold" reaction to those—to the tune of $12–$20 per check, and the vendors to whom you bounced the check may charge you $25 for that check. Suddenly, whatever you bought costs you $40 more! Hey, you're in college, so you're pretty smart, right? Spending $40 more per bounced check is not very smart, right? Right.

C'MON. . .IT'S EASY!

Now, to actually balance the checkbook. Having a computer program (such as Quicken) can make the job very easy. But, you can also do the old-fashioned route with pencil and calculator using the handy-dandy steps on the back of your bank statement. (You *do* need to open the bank statement.) Compare your check register with each transaction recorded by the bank.

CATCH A CLUE

Tips for Keeping Track

1. Get duplicate checks. Otherwise, at least write the amount in the register.
2. Keep all ATM receipts in a section of your checkbook to be recorded as soon as possible.
3. Keep all debit-card receipts to be recorded as soon as possible.

Subtract from your checkbook balance any you might have missed (perhaps you forgot to record an ATM transaction or forgot to include the ATM charges), as well as any bank service charges or (heaven forbid!) overdraft fees. Record everything and get a final balance in your check register before you move on.

FOR COMPUTER USERS

If you have a computer, you can get software that will help you with this process. A program, such as Quicken, has a check register in which you enter all transactions. Then it does the calculations for you. A special button on your task bar will start a program to reconcile your checkbook and walk you through it step-by-step. Not having to enter all numbers on a calculator can save on errors and make the whole process go faster. Another fun thing about a computer program for your checkbook is that it can help you with a budget. Also, as you enter each check, you will be asked to give it a category. Then, at any point you can see how much you're spending each month on gas, pizza, and movies. This can be a big help as you plan or try to stay on a budget. And it's fast and relatively painless!

KEEP GOING

Checks that have been written but have not yet cleared the bank will be totaled and placed in the appropriate space on the back of your bank statement. These are called "outstanding" checks—no, not "amazing" checks, they are just still *out*. (There may be some from pre-

Money Wisdom

DON'T FORGET

"The earnings of the godly enhance their lives, but evil people squander their money on sin."

(Proverbs 10:16 NLT)

vious months, so make sure you get them all.) Finally, you'll add up the outstanding checks; then add the final amount you have in your checkbook and get a subtotal.

Next, match up all the deposits. Again, recent deposits may not be on the statement, so these will be totaled and placed in the appropriate space on the back of your bank statement. Total the outstanding deposits; then add to that number the ending balance as shown on your bank statement for a final total.

When you've finished the formula on the back of the statement, ideally the final numbers on your worksheet and in your checkbook register will match. If they don't match, patiently go back and redo all the steps and double-check your math in the register. It may take some time, but you'll find your mistake so that you can know your bottom line.

For better or worse, that's how much money you have. *Don't* overspend! In fact, it helps to have a budget to keep yourself on track.

THE BIG B

You need it. . .you really can't survive without it. No, not a home-cooked meal (although that would be good), but a *budget*.

A budget is your spending guideline. It helps you stay on track and not run out of money before you run out of month.

WIDE ANGLE

Budget 101

To set up a budget, first list all of your expenses. Here's an example; you will need to adjust yours for your personal needs. (Keep in mind that some of these fees may have to be paid in full at the beginning of each semester, so "Books and supplies" may not need to be included in your monthly budget. If you are living and eating off campus, then you will have to budget these expenses on a per-month basis.)

Tuition and fees
Food (over and above meal plan)
Other school fees
Housing
Utilities
Room furnishings
Meal plan
Tithe
Telephone
Transportation
Car payment/gas/insurance
Bus fare
Savings

For next semester
For medical expenses
For car repairs
Clothing
Personal needs (shampoo, soap)
Laundry
Entertainment
Other monthly payments
Credit Cards

A NOTE ABOUT GIVING

You need to think of your tithe as a bill you pay with each paycheck (although no one comes collecting if you *don't* pay, and there's no interest added when you're late). Jesus was clear that His people ought to give. Giving was instituted for God's people so that they would always keep their money and possessions in perspective. It is the same for us today. It is proportional giving. It is money given so that we can help God's kingdom do its work in the world. In fact, if we refuse to give, God says we're actually robbing Him (Malachi 3:8). He gives us 100 percent; if we refuse to give any back, then it does amount to robbery! But in turn, God promises that if we are faithful in the foundational discipline of tithing, He will be faithful to meet all our needs (Malachi 3:10–12).

MAKE IT YOURS

When you have decided what categories your expenses will be in, make a sheet that you can photocopy. Use one copy to write down your best guess as far as what you will need. (First-year students may need to ask some seasoned veterans for their advice—but don't ask any guys about laundry expenses.) Use the other copies on a month-to-month basis to keep track of what you're spending in various categories. This will also help you to see when you need to cut back in a particular area. Keeping these sheets will also help you to make sure you're remembering all the bills you need to pay each month. Look at the bills that actually require monthly payments (such as a car payment or credit-card payment), check the due dates, and make sure you get those payments in on time each month.

Great Quotes on Money

wow! "Money never made a man happy yet, nor will it. There is nothing in its nature to produce happiness. The more a man has, the more he wants. That was a true proverb of the wise man, rely upon it: 'Better is little with the fear of the Lord, than great treasure, and trouble therewith.' "
—Benjamin Franklin

"Make all you can, save all you can, give all you can." —John Wesley

"The making of money is necessary for daily living, but money-making is apt to degenerate into money-loving, and then the deceitfulness of riches enters in and spoils our spiritual life."
—Billy Graham

Depending on how you're financing your education, whether you are working for a paycheck once or twice a month, or whether you have a chunk of savings from summer that has to last, you must make a budget plan that works. You may need to make some adjustments along the way (for example, maybe you won't need as much food money as you thought—or maybe you'll need *more*). But make the budget work for *you*. You'll be glad you did.

IT WORKS!

Going to college with a budget in hand and a checkbook that makes sense can take two big unknowns out of the picture. In addition, you're developing skills that will last you a lifetime—you will always need to know how much money you have, and you'll always need a budget. You'll find that it works!

The Credit-Card Trap

PLAYING WITH PLASTIC

Credit cards! So magical, so easy to use, so portable. . .so deadly! Chances are, if you're a college student, every credit-card company in the country has sent you those shiny pieces of plastic. If you feel that you need a card, look past all the great offers and read the fine print. Does the card have an annual fee? If they're offering a low introductory rate, make sure the rate doesn't sky-rocket after the first few months. Try to find those that offer a grace period.

If you're going to take a card off to college with you, be sure you can handle the temptation. Decide ahead of time what expenses the card will be for—and don't use it for anything else! Put it in a place where you have

WIDE ANGLE

Warning

"I do not believe credit cards are sinful, but they are dangerous. Americans carry over 700 million of them, and only 30 percent of their charge accounts are paid in full each month. It has been statistically shown that people spend approximately one-third more when they use credit cards rather than cash. Here's the rule of thumb: If you always pay the entire monthly balance due, you can probably handle your credit cards. If you do not, they are too dangerous for you. In that case, I suggest you perform plastic surgery—any good pair of scissors will do."
—Howard Dayton, from "How to Get Out of Debt," in *Husbands and Wives*

to work to get to it. This will keep you from running up huge amounts of debt—and believe me, it can happen fast!

Savings Chart

BEGIN NOW

You probably don't have a lot of money to save. But if you can skimp by without some luxuries now, you'll be able to enjoy many more later. Look at the facts below.

If you save $2,000 a year from ages 21–25 then stop saving,

you could have more money at
age 65 than the person who
saves $2,000 every year between
the ages 26-64.

It's Amazing

Compound interest
has been called the
Eighth Wonder of
the Modern World.

WOW!

How can this be? It all comes
down to interest. By saving early,
the interest you earn begins
accumulating sooner. Then the interest you earn *on that interest*
accumulates sooner, and so on. In a short time the money you
earn on your *interest* is greater than the money you invest each
year. The chart below illustrates the point. Even if you might not
have $2,000 to put away today, you can begin by putting *something* away.

Age	Investment: Early Starter	Investment: Late Starter
21	$2,000	$0
22	$2,000	$0
23	$2,000	$0
24	$2,000	$0
25	$2,000	$0
26	$0	$2,000
27	$0	$2,000
28	$0	$2,000
29	$0	$2,000
30	$0	$2,000
31	$0	$2,000
32	$0	$2,000
33	$0	$2,000
34	$0	$2,000
35	$0	$2,000
36	$0	$2,000
37	$0	$2,000
38	$0	$2,000
39	$0	$2,000
40	$0	$2,000
41	$0	$2,000
42	$0	$2,000
43	$0	$2,000

Age	Investment: Early Starter	Investment: Late Starter
44	$0	$2,000
45	$0	$2,000
46	$0	$2,000
47	$0	$2,000
48	$0	$2,000
49	$0	$2,000
50	$0	$2,000
51	$0	$2,000
52	$0	$2,000
53	$0	$2,000
54	$0	$2,000
55	$0	$2,000
56	$0	$2,000
57	$0	$2,000
58	$0	$2,000
59	$0	$2,000
60	$0	$2,000
61	$0	$2,000
62	$0	$2,000
63	$0	$2,000
64	$0	$2,000

Total out-of-pocket money you invested

$10,000 $78,000

Total savings based on annual return of 15 percent

$3,612,075.63 $3,558,180.62

Section 7
Being a Christian College Student

Being a Christian College Student

BEING A CHRISTIAN ON A SECULAR CAMPUS

You've seen the movie. Dorothy wants to run away from her boring life on the farm and find adventure and excitement in faraway lands. She gets her wish, sort of, arriving via a dream in the magical and mysterious land of Oz. It's there and then, staring at her strange, surreal surroundings, that she utters the immortal phrase, "Toto, I have a feeling we're not in Kansas anymore."

Perhaps there's no better description of how many Christian students feel when they first set foot on a secular campus. Even though they've heard the stories, even though they've seen movies like *Animal House*, the differences between a Christian environment and a secular-university setting are stark (and often unsettling).

SOME DIFFERENCES BETWEEN CHRISTIAN AND SECULAR SCHOOLS

	Christian	Secular
Welcome week	Video of summer mission trips	Personal appearance by "Condom Man"
Campus movies	Movies!? Don't you know movies are sinful!	*Showgirls; La Dolce Vita* (with subtitles)
Campus concert	Steven Curtis Chapman	R.E.M.
Typical activity	Prayer in the quad; coed soccer in the gym	Streaking in the quad; moshing at Muther's (an off-campus bar)
Typical roommate	Pat, whose parents are missionaries in Nairobi, Kenya, and who reads Oswald Chambers every night	Terry, whose parents divorced 12 years ago, and who has three tattoos (visible) and smokes two packs a day

	Christian	**Secular**
Typical commencement speaker	Chuck Colson, James Dobson	Sharon Stone, Hillary Clinton
Campus concerns	Littering, riding bikes on sidewalks	Arson, rape, illegal drug use, student suicide
Typical dorm decor	Bible verses taped to mirror over sink, African violet on windowsill	*Penthouse* foldouts on walls, marijuana growing in lighted terrarium in closet
Classes	New Testament Intro, World Missions	Pop Culture 101, American Cinema since 1960
Protest	Petition over too much fatty food in the cafeteria	Takeover of administration because of not enough nonwhite lesbian professors on the faculty
Bumper sticker	"Our God is an AWESOME God!"	"Party naked"

Such differences raise some important issues and questions:

Should a Christian Attend a Secular University?

This is not a simple, black-and-white issue. There are educational concerns. Some secular schools offer the best (or only) programs in certain fields. There are financial considerations. Many students simply do not have the economic means to pay for schooling at a private Christian institution. There are long-term, "real life" factors to ponder. Christian students who have been extremely sheltered all

The Lie

"Many of you young persons out there are seriously thinking about going to college. (That is, of course, a lie. The only things you young persons think seriously about are loud music and beer. Trust me: these are closely related to college.)"—Dave Barry

wow!

of their lives (e.g., homeschooled and/or K–12 in a Christian school and then four years at a Christian college) are sometimes ill prepared to suddenly move out into a secular environment. There's also the biblical imperative of missions. By that we're referring to God's global purpose of seeing His name glorified through the proclamation of the gospel of Christ throughout the earth. In short, God wants to use us to draw others to Himself. One great place to do this is at a secular university. A person can pursue a college degree and, at the same time, be "salt and light" (Matthew 5:13–16) in a needy mission field not far from home.

A TRUE STORY (BELIEVE IT OR NOT!)

A college freshman at the University of Arkansas banded together with another Christian friend or two and pledged Sigma Alpha Epsilon (a social fraternity). This particular fraternity was notorious for its wild-and-crazy reputation. But these young Christian men were on a mission. They began praying for their "brothers." They modeled the Christian life and shared their faith. Four years later, when these men graduated, there were some 50-60 Christians in the chapter!

Can Christians really make a difference? Obviously we can!

Will My Faith Suffer at a Secular University?

It certainly can! There are huge temptations everywhere (even at Christian colleges), but in a secular college setting, the enticements are anything but subtle. Rampant, open immorality. Constant partying. Worldly conversations. A glaring censorship of all things Christian. Such is the atmosphere on most secular campuses.

Even so, it's possible not merely to survive, but to thrive. Tens of thousands of Christians are growing in their faith and serving God and making an enormous difference at secular universities!

LIVE AN EXEMPLARY, GODLY LIFE

The more convinced we are of our true identity in Christ, the more our behavior will show it. When we are "blown away" by God's love for us, the overwhelming desire of our hearts is to love Him in return (and to show that love by a life of trust and obedience).

Look at Peter's description (1 Peter 2:9–12). We will be:

- "a people. . .[who] declare the praises of [God]"—worship will be our lifestyle (and not just something we do on Sunday mornings). Our lives will be marked by joy and celebration at all God has done and is doing in us, through us, and for us.

- people who "abstain from sinful desires"—because of the Holy Spirit dwelling within us, we have the power to say "No!" to devilish temptations and sins. We know that such things, though appealing and alluring, are actually deadly. They represent Satan's "war against [our] soul." And though our old nature might desire such things, our new, true nature longs for the things of God.

Live Up to Your Identity

DON'T FORGET

"But you are a chosen people, a royal priesthood, a holy nation, a people belonging to God, that you may declare the praises of Him who called you out of darkness into His wonderful light. Once you were not a people, but now you are the people of God; once you had not received mercy, but now you have received mercy.

Dear friends, I urge you, as aliens and strangers in the world, to abstain from sinful desires, which war against your soul. Live such good lives among the pagans that, though they accuse you of doing wrong, they may see your good deeds and glorify God on the day He visits us." (I Peter 2:9–12)

- people who "live. . .good lives among the pagans. . .[and do] good deeds"—in contrast to those who live for self, we will live for Christ. Our lives will be marked by kindness and compassion. In an evil world, we will stand out. And the result is that God will ultimately be glorified. Only He could work such a change in our hearts.

Being a Christian on a secular campus is a difficult calling. But it is possible to embrace this challenge and be successful. What's more, you don't have to go it alone. Keep reading for some further insight on how to find the help you'll need to succeed in a hostile environment.

Also in this section, you'll find some practical tips for beefing up your own walk with God.

Choosing a Church

When it comes to church, Christian college students cover the spectrum. Meet four typical students:

Ned Nonattender. Ned's rationale for his unwillingness to go to church? "Hey, I'm already involved in a Christian group on campus that meets during the week. We worship and study the Bible there. Plus, God's not just in some building at a certain time each week! Some Sunday mornings I like to get up early and go play golf. The course isn't crowded, and I can really talk to God while I'm out there."

Mary Meanswell. Every week Mary unleashes a new flurry of promises and good intentions. She tells friends she really *is* going to attend church with them. Definitely. This Sunday. No kidding. Watch. You'll see. But then she stays up late on Saturday watching videos in the dorm. And when the alarm sounds on Sunday, she can't (read: *won't*) pull herself out of bed.

Fred Fickle. Fred's all over the map. One Sunday he's at First. The next week he's someplace else. If the music or sermon doesn't suit him one place, he's across town the following week. Fred's what you call a church hopper. If he's not careful, he'll go four years and never land anywhere.

Carla Committed. Carla spent her first semester at college visiting most of the local churches. She asked a lot of questions, prayed about what to do, and then actually JOINED **one** particular congregation. That's where she goes, serves, and gives—faithfully. She's a *member,* not just an *attender.* And at least from the outside looking in, she's having the best church experience by far.

ADVANTAGES OF GETTING PLUGGED IN

The confidence of knowing that you are associated with a local "chapter" of the only institution on earth that Christ promised to build and bless: His Church!

• Steady spiritual growth

• Preaching of God's Word

• Exposure to older, wiser Christians

- Career role models
- Marital role models
- Parenting role models
- A wide range of opportunities for service (using your spiritual gifts)
- A chance to impact younger kids
- Participation in the ordinances of the church (Lord's Supper, baptism)
- Intergenerational worship and fellowship
- Doctrinal and moral accountability
- A safety net when times get tough (and they will!)
- A family/home away from your real family/home. And if you play your cards right . . .
- Possible free meals and laundry privileges from families who recognize you as a member of the body!

About Church

DON'T FORGET

"The church is not a department store where you come and get the spiritual commodity you want, then go your way. To speak of loving Christ, while neglecting His body, the church (Ephesians 1:23; 4:12, 15–16; 5:29–30) is hypocritical."
—Donald Whitney

Staying Focused on God

The history of God's people reveals, among other things, that we are forgetful, easily distracted people. "Prone to wander, Lord, I feel it; prone to leave the God I love" is the way the old hymn puts it. It's not difficult to see why this is true. With worldly enticements and devilish temptations from *without*, and fleshly desires churning *within*, it's a huge battle to stay focused on God and to keep walking with Him.

In recognition of this human frailty, the Bible says much about remembering. (Note: The word *remember* is found 166 times in the NIV Bible, along with numerous admonitions to *not forget* God!) Old Testament saints made it a common practice to bring to mind God's great acts in their festivals and psalms. They often erected monuments to commemorate divine encounters and deliverances. In the New Testament we find similar customs, the most obvious being Christ's institution of the Lord's Supper. This simple meal of wine and bread was intended by Jesus to be celebrated regularly so that believers would be reminded often of Christ (His sacrifice, His presence, His coming again).

GREAT BIBLE PASSAGES ABOUT FOCUSING ON GOD

"When you have eaten and are satisfied, praise the LORD your God for the good land He has given you. Be careful that you do not forget the LORD your God, failing to observe His commands, His laws and His decrees that I am giving you this day. Otherwise, when you eat and are satisfied, when you build fine houses and settle down, and when your herds and flocks grow large and your silver and gold increase and all you have is multiplied, then your heart will become proud and you will forget the LORD your God." (Deuteronomy 8:10–14)

"But seek first His kingdom and His righteousness, and all these things will be given to you as well." (Matthew 6:33)

"Let us fix our eyes on Jesus, the author and perfecter of our faith." (Hebrews 12:2)

"Set your minds on things above, not on earthly things." (Colossians 3:2)

"What is more, I consider everything a loss compared to the surpassing greatness of knowing Christ Jesus my Lord, for whose sake I have lost all things. I consider them rubbish, that I may gain Christ." (Philippians 3:8)

"So we fix our eyes not on what is seen, but on what is unseen. For what is seen is temporary, but what is unseen is eternal." (2 Corinthians 4:18)

"By faith Moses, when he had grown up, refused to be known as the son of Pharaoh's daughter. He chose to be mistreated along with the people of God rather than to enjoy the pleasures of sin for a short time. He regarded disgrace for the sake of Christ as of greater value than the treasures of Egypt, because he was looking ahead to his reward. By faith he left Egypt, not fearing the king's anger; he persevered because he saw Him who is invisible." (Hebrews 11:24–27)

RESOURCES THAT CAN HELP US STAY FOCUSED ON GOD

Christian Friends
Ecclesiastes 4:9–10 says:

> "Two are better than one, because they have a good return for their work: If one falls down, his friend can help him up. But pity the man who falls and has no one to help him up!"

How true this is! We all need a person or two in our lives who knows us, loves us, and, most importantly, shares our desire to walk with God.

Involvement in Campus Ministry
Almost every campus in the world (unless you're going to Agnostic State U or Lucifer Beelzebub College) has at least one or two active Christian groups. In your college town, look for a church with an established campus ministry. Or find an organization like Campus Crusade for Christ, InterVarsity Christian Fellowship, Student Mobilization, Reformed University Fellowship, the Navigators, Fellowship of Christian Athletes, the BSU (Baptist Student Union), Chi Alpha (Assemblies of God), etc.

These kinds of parachurch organizations should not *take the place of church* in your life, but they can enhance your walk and help you grow in your faith.

Church
As mentioned in the previous chapter, faithful church involvement (not just sporadic attendance) can be a tremendous help to us spiritually.

Personal Disciplines
It's a great thing to be surrounded by other believers who are

challenging you spiritually and helping keep you focused. It's *not* a good thing to depend *entirely* upon such external resources for your spiritual health. You also need to be developing an internal spiritual focus that will keep you on target during those times in life when you're not surrounded by Christian influences.

The single best way to develop a godward mind-set and focus is to begin the practice of spending time with God every day. Whether you call this practice having devotions, a quiet time, or a daily appointment with God, the idea is to get alone with the Lord and spend time talking to and listening to Him. It's during this time that you shove worldly distractions and trivial concerns from your mind, and bring to mind the things that are true—about God, about you, about the world, about the purpose of life.

The Christians who are persistent in doing this are far more likely to stay focused on God. The believers who neglect this practice (and depend solely on an occasional sermon or Christian gathering to keep them strong) are the ones who are likely to drift away from God. This topic will be covered in more detail in the section entitled "How to Grow Spiritually."

Scripture Memory and Meditation
The psalmist wrote,

> "I have hidden Your word in my heart that I might not sin against You" (Psalm 119:11).

Here's the bottom line of what that verse means: When we store God's truth (i.e., His Word) in our hearts and minds, and when we make it our practice to meditate upon that truth, we stay on track spiritually.

Meditation is not some passive Eastern practice where we sit cross-legged and hum quietly. It's an active process of bringing scriptural truth to mind, thinking hard about it, and examining it from every angle. The more we ponder, reflect, cogitate on the Word, the more chance it has to seep into our souls. Over time, these biblical truths move from being "nice ideas" to "bedrock convictions." Our attitudes change. Our values are shaped into the very values of God.

Finding Support

In college the question isn't *"Will* I encounter tough times?" Nope. The more accurate way to phrase it is, *"When* will I encounter tough times, and *what sort of* trials will they be?"

REAL TRIALS OF COLLEGIATES

- New and difficult academic challenges ("This ain't high school!")

- Financial shortfalls ("I've got no more plasma to sell!")

- Relational breakups and heartaches ("He wants to date my roommate!")

- Roommate problems ("What a slob!")

- Changes in relating to parents ("I'm trying to grow up, and they're still treating me like a kid!")

- Transportation nightmares ("Bumming rides. . .what a bummer!")

- Career/choice of major crises ("What do I want to be when I grow up?")

- Social traumas ("Why can't I—get a date/find a friend/etc.?")

- Family emergencies ("My mom just called to tell me—my granddad died/she's leaving my dad/my dad lost his job!")

Imagined Trials of Collegiates

THE BOTTOM LINE

Not enough sleep[1]
Not enough to eat[2]
Not enough Starbucks[3]
Not enough entertainment[4]
Not enough parties[5]
Not enough interaction with the opposite sex[6]
Not enough time to study[7]

[1] The problem here is one of discipline. Check your schedule again.
[2] Free or very cheap food is available everywhere; you just have to know where to look.
[3] You may not be able to find the real deal, but you can always find a cheaper imitation.
[4] No sympathy here. This generation offers more amusement than at any time in history. The key is creativity.
[5] What?! Everybody knows college is one extended four-year party. (Five years for a few smart, lucky souls!)
[6] You must be at an all-girl school or in a REAL major.
[7] Pleeeeeeeezzzzzeee! Give us a break. The issue isn't time; it's time *management*.

- A quantum leap in worldly temptations ("Everywhere I turn it's sex, drugs—or beer—and rock and roll!")

- Self-made messes ("Why didn't I study ahead? Why did I make the choice to date him?")

Possible Support Systems

Clearly, you're going to need a good support system. A safety net. And you also (on a more positive note) need good role models.
Consider joining:

- A small group

- A church

- An adoptive family

Quit Complaining

DON'T FORGET

"College students are the only people in the world who: receive huge family and/or government subsidies, have all their meals cooked for them, have all their dishes washed for them, have their bathrooms cleaned regularly for them, get 10–12 hours of sleep per day, have, at most, four to six hours a day of actual responsibility, have almost un-limited time to goof off, and who... COMPLAIN ABOUT HOW HARD AND AWFUL THEIR LIVES ARE!"
—Author unknown

How to Grow Spiritually (Bible Study, Prayer)

Quiz o' the Day!

Fact: The New Testament indicates that our outer actions are a good measure of our inner spiritual health (Matthew 7:16–20).

Question: What could we conclude about someone who:

- Watches only religious movies like *The Ten Commandments*

- Memorizes the Gospel of Matthew (in Greek)

- Reads the complete works of C. S. Lewis annually

- Shares the *Four Spiritual Laws* with strangers in airports

- Preaches with a bullhorn at downtown bus stops
- Fasts during the Thanksgiving break
- Goes to all three Sunday services so he can take communion three times
- Gives her entire paycheck to missionaries in Malawi
- Throws his TV out the dorm window and pledges to read only the Bible
- Spends vacations and breaks working at an inner-city soup kitchen?

Answer: Nothing! External actions alone do not necessarily indicate spiritual life, health, or growth. (If you don't believe it, just consider the Pharisees in the Gospels.)

Confused? Keep reading!

Spiritual Life and Spiritual Growth

In the physical realm, from the moment we are born we begin a long process of physical growth. We learn to crawl, climb, splash around in the toilet (yeehaw!), walk, talk, take care of ourselves (at least theoretically), etc. Such growth is normal, natural, and expected. A failure to develop in this manner is an indication of sickness and/or retardation (picture a college freshman in diapers and sucking a pacifier!).

It's important to realize that a similar process is also at work in the spiritual realm. We are "born again" (John 3:1–21) when we put our faith in Christ. As new believers we are, in a very real sense, spiritual infants who need to grow up. When we do *not* grow spiritually, something is deeply wrong.

The Components of Growth

Physical growth requires proper nutrition plus exercise plus time. Guess what? It's the same in the spiritual realm. Growing spiritually requires a healthy intake of God's Word (hearing it taught, reading it, studying it, memorizing it, meditating upon it) and a commitment to exercise our faith daily through prayer, service, witnessing, etc. Spiritual growth takes time. We'll have some "growth spurts" (just as we do in the physical realm) where we seem to take big leaps forward. But by and large, our spiritual growth will be slow and almost imperceptible.

MOTIVES FOR GROWTH

Some Christians fall into a kind of selfish pride when it comes to spiritual growth. More than wanting to grow so that they can know God better, glorify Him more fully, and serve Him more effectively, they actually want to grow so they can impress other people. For these few, the real goal is to be perceived as "godly." This explains their zeal for Scripture memory or deep Bible study. Sometimes a secret competition can even develop between believers as they vie for the title of "most spiritually mature." Check your own motives for wanting to grow. Are you just eager to be and do what God wants, or is there a hidden agenda in your heart?

OBSTACLES TO GROWTH

Some believers are spiritually malnourished. They erroneously think they can get by on a minimum of true spiritual food. Guess what? A sermon here, a few verses there, or a Bible promise every once in awhile won't cut it. That's a kind of "spiritual anorexia"! No one can thrive living like that.

Still other believers settle for "processed and packaged" spiritual food. That is they opt for a diet of Christian books and magazine articles. While such materials aren't necessarily *bad*, they can never measure up to the "100-percent (super)natural" goodness of the pure Word of God. It's like the difference in bland, canned corn that has been stripped of most of its vitamins and that you end up putting artificial margarine on, and fresh, right-off-the-stalk corn-on-the-cob that you slather real butter on. . . SO sweet and crunchy and fresh. . . .

The point? If you're spending more time reading books *about the Bible*, than you are actually reading *the Bible itself*, you'll never grow as much or as fast as you otherwise could.

How to Witness without Beating Someone over the Head

If you're on a secular campus, you're guaranteed to encounter (daily!) people who are spiritually clueless and who need, more than anything else in the world, to meet Jesus Christ. How do you tell them without being offensive?

THE SEVEN HABITS OF HIGHLY EFFECTIVE WITNESSES

1. See the Good News as GOOD NEWS!

When good things happen to us, it's natural for us to tell everyone we see! No one ever has to say, "Now that you're engaged, Cindi, and wearing a 1.8 carat diamond ring on your left hand, I want to encourage and challenge you to go out and tell people." Isn't that a crazy notion? And yet Christians have to be prodded and pushed to share their faith! Why?

Maybe it is because we have forgotten what the gospel really means.

We Were	But Now We Are
Lost	Found
Spiritually dead	Spiritually alive
In darkness	In the light
Captives of Satan	Children of God
Guilty	Forgiven
Under God's wrath	Surrounded by God's love
Unrighteous	Righteous in Christ
Without real meaning in life	The possessors of an eternal purpose
Headed for hell	Promised heaven

The more we reflect on what our salvation really means, the more excited we will be!

2. Remember That Evangelism Is a Lifestyle.

Evangelism isn't something we *do*. It's something we *are*, twenty-four hours a day, seven days a week. Don't be a commando evangelist, who sets aside one hour a week for witnessing raids. Ask God each morning to give you occasions (and the necessary sensitivity to those opportunities) to share with others the reason for the hope that is within you (1 Peter 3:15). Do it in the dorm, in the cafeteria, in the intramural complex.

3. Remember That Evangelism Is a Process.

We're not just trying to get converts, we're trying to make disciples (Matthew 28:18–20). This can include anything from getting a friend to see that there actually are good reasons for believing in a personal God (a process sometimes called pre-evangelism) to explaining why Christ had to die on the cross. Don't limit your thinking to merely sharing a gospel tract. Evangelism is *much* broader than that.

4. Remember to "Show and Tell."

Good witnessing involves a delicate balance between *showing* others the reality of the gospel (with our lives) and *telling* them the content of the gospel (with our lips). If there's no demonstration, our words lack credibility. Without words, there's no clear explanation for our changed lives.

5. Be Filled with the Spirit.

In the book of Acts, the filling of the Spirit was always followed by outreach. Acts 1:8 is the strongest reminder that we *must* have God's Spirit controlling and empowering us (Ephesians 5:18) if we are to be powerful and effective witnesses. Does God have YOUR whole heart?

6. Be Honest and Natural.

Forget about canned approaches and memorized speeches. Just be yourself. Don't pretend to be what you're not, but also don't hide who you really are. Talk about how God has changed you, how He helps you through struggles. If you're real, people will be drawn to you and your Lord, not repelled.

7. Leave the Results to God.

We can't save anyone. All we can do is faithfully deliver the message. It's up to God to work in His timing. Remembering that truth can save us much worry and heartache.

Section 8
Friendships and Dating

The Buddy System

CHOOSING FRIENDS

Let's assume that you're starting college alone, that you're not rooming with your best friend from high school, that your older sister doesn't live in the dorm next door, and that you're not fifteen minutes away from the neighborhood where you grew up. It's just you—for now.

What you've got is a blank friendship slate. And while that may seem depressing to you, don't reach for the Kleenex box just yet. (We don't mean to suggest that all of your old friends back home have vanished from the face of the earth. Of course you still have friends. We're talking about having people to share the adventure of college with you. If you don't have anybody who fits that bill yet, you have a blank friendship slate.)

Do you remember the last time you had a blank friendship slate, the opportunity to start relationships from scratch? Was it high school? Did you know anyone when you started ninth grade? Was it junior high? Do you even remember a time when you had no one to hang out with?

The reason we ask is that there's a certain freedom that goes along with a blank friendship slate. You're not restricted by cliques, stereotypes, or the opinions of others from getting to know the people you want to know. You don't have to worry about being seen with someone. You don't have to concern yourself with how your popularity will be affected if you're friends with geeks, jocks, punks, or artsy types.

You've got a blank slate to fill any way you want. Here are some things you might want to consider when you start choosing friends in college.

DIVERSIFY YOUR RELATIONSHIPS

The college experience is made up of several different components: classes, dorm life, work, extracurricular activities, and so forth. Work toward establishing a group of friends in each of these areas.

Classes

First, there are your classes. Obvious choices here would be people in your major. Look for familiar faces in the classroom, people with whom you have more than one class. Once you've identified three or four such folks, strike up conversations with them by asking what they think of the classes, the professors, and the homework. Talk about why you chose the major and what you plan to do when you get out of school. Make it a point to sit together in your classes and work together on projects. Few things relieve the drudgery of going to class quicker than seeing the smiling face of a friend saving a seat for you.

Dorm Life

The second component is dorm life. The place to start this friendship search is within the walls of your own room. Freshman roommate pairings are a guessing game. You never know what you're going to get. If it turns out that you and your roommate share similar interests, personality types, and personal habits, give thanks. Nothing is better than a roommate who also happens to be a good friend. But don't count on that happening. Rooming together carries with it a whole lot of baggage that can get in the way of friendship. If you and your roomie aren't tight, don't sweat it. You've got a whole floor full of people to get to know.

One of the great things about dorm life is that people tend to advertise their personalities, hobbies, and interests on their walls. Walking from your room to the bathroom, you could see or hear maybe five or six areas of common ground in the rooms you pass. One room might have a poster of Groucho Marx on the wall. If you love the Marx Brothers' movies, stop by and mention it. Another room might have Elvis Costello blasting from the stereo. If *Imperial Bedroom* is your all-time favorite album, stop by and compliment the person on her taste in music. A third room might have a soccer net draped from wall to wall. If you played in high school, stop by and swap game stories. The potential for common interests is endless. Add those common interests to the fact that you'll be living on the same floor for a year, and you've got the makings of a potential friendship.

Work

The third component of college life is work. If you need to earn money at school and you're looking for friends, it only makes sense that you should choose a job that allows you to work with others. Whether it's with a campus landscaping crew or at a local pizza joint, your job can introduce you to several potential friends.

The good thing about making friends with the people at work is that you don't have to find an excuse to get close to them. You're stuck with your coworkers. You're together and you've got a job to do, so you might as well make the best of it.

What most people are looking for at work is someone to make the job a little more fun or to make the time go a little faster. Can you be that kind of a person? We're not talking about goofing off here. You're being paid to do a job, so do it, and do it well. But whenever possible, enjoy yourself and help others enjoy themselves. From such simple pleasures, friendships are formed.

Extracurricular Activities

The fourth component of college life is extracurricular activities. These might include anything from sports to rock bands to political causes to volunteer work. Of all the components of college life, this one lends itself most easily to friendships. Your involvement in an extracurricular activity signals your interest in it. The same holds true for everyone else involved. Voila! Instant common ground.

Are you athletically inclined? Sign up for an

CATCH A CLUE

Defy Stereotypes

With a blank friendship slate, you've got nothing to lose. Now is the best time for you to see how the other half lives. So gather up your courage and start talking to people who obviously have different priorities, backgrounds, and outlooks on life than you do.

If you see someone dressed in black leather with bands of metal spikes around his wrist and neck eating alone in the dining hall, sit down at his table and strike up a conversation. Don't allow your preconceived notions to dictate how you act with the person. Don't be intimidated. Talk about the things you would talk about with so-called "normal" people. Ask him about classes, where he's from, and how he likes school. If you're curious about why he dresses the way he does, ask him about it—but don't be condescending. You may be surprised at the person you find underneath the leather and spikes.

intramural team and make friends in the heat of competition. Or spend some time in the weight room and find a lifting partner. Or advertise for a racquetball partner on the campus bulletin board.

Are you politically minded? Talk to local officials about helping with voter registration, campaigning, or some other aspect of the democratic process. Watch for other volunteers from the campus. On campus, volunteer your services to a candidate running for student-body president. Make it a point to get to know your fellow workers.

How Do You Handle a Social Leech?

The best way to handle a leech is to explain to him exactly how you're feeling—in the kindest way possible. Pull the person aside and have a heart-to-heart talk with him. Say something like, "Look, I need some personal space. It seems as if we're spending every day together, and that's just not my style. There are times when I want to get together with some of my other friends without anyone else around. Do you know what I'm talking about?" The confrontation is likely to hurt his feelings, but if you're honest and compassionate, he should get the message.

One Is the Loneliest Number

How to Handle Loneliness

Loneliness is the Achilles' heel of many college freshmen. The classes don't get them, the dining-hall food doesn't get them, the professors don't get them, bad roommates don't even get them. But the loneliness gets them. That gnawing, terrifying feeling of being alone, the only person within a hundred miles who knows or cares that you exist. The stomach-churning fear that you'll never connect with anyone on campus and that you're staring four years of solitary life

Hmmm...

"Yes, they're sharing a drink they call loneliness, but it's better than drinking alone."—Billy Joel, "Piano Man"

WIDE ANGLE

in the face. That's what gets college freshmen.

EVERYBODY HURTS

Imagine that you could somehow cut away the outer wall of a college dorm and observe the cross section of what goes on inside. What you would see? (Okay, okay, we know what you'd *see,* but that's not what we're talking about.) What you would see are dozens of lonely people suffering alone. You'd see Lindsay ironing her clothes for next week. You'd see Mya writing e-mail messages to her sister back home. You'd see Steph cutting out pictures for her roommate's birthday card, even though her roommate's birthday is six weeks away. You'd see Ki watching TV. You'd see Callie strumming her guitar. You'd see Keisha praying for a friend. It's Friday night, and you'd see that three of the girls are crying.

One of the nastiest little secrets among college freshmen on campuses today is that most of them are lonely. The bitter irony is that it's loneliness, and the self-focus and self-pity that goes along with it, that keeps them from recognizing each other's pain.

Another devastating secret is that loneliness is a natural *re*action to a lack of healthy *inter*action. Psychiatrist Frederick W. Coons suggested that one of the primary tasks a student performs in college is coming to terms with his or her need for intimacy. College-age young people have a tremendous need for the closeness and sharing that comes from intimacy with another person. Usually the person they seek intimacy with is of the same sex. It must be made clear, however, that this intimacy is *not* sexual in nature. (Some people make the mistake of believing it is and become confused sexually.) Instead, it's the intimacy that comes when personal feelings and needs are shared with someone who can serve as an encourager. It's the cornerstone of a lifelong friendship. Where loneliness exists, though, intimacy cannot. Intro to Loneliness—now there's a freshmen class that would fill up in no time flat. The professor would walk to the podium, look out at the class, gesture to everyone in the room with a sweeping motion of his arm, and say, "Everybody in this room is lonely. Help each other." Then he'd dismiss the class for the semester, because that's all the students would need to know.

WAGING A WAR ON LONELINESS

Loneliness is the enemy of college freshmen, and this enemy must be destroyed! What's more, *you* may be the person to help destroy it on your campus! If that sounds too ambitious for you, how would you feel about becoming the point person for an assault on loneliness in your dorm? If that's still a bit much, do you have what it takes to bring together the lonely people on your *floor?* We're betting you do.

Your first step is simply a matter of making contact. It's a Friday night and everyone who's going out is out. It's time for you to start knocking on some doors. Go up and down the hall and invite everyone left on the floor to your room for some hot chocolate and some of your mom's homemade molasses cookies that you received in a care package. Some people will jump at your offer; others may be a little reluctant (even in the midst of loneliness, shyness is a hard thing to overcome). Don't be a pest about it, but really encourage people to accept your invitation.

Once you've got everybody together, spend some time getting to know each other. Encourage everyone in the room to talk about where she's from, what she's majoring in, yada, yada, yada. What you talk about isn't nearly as important as the fact that you've got people to talk to. Before your little party breaks up, invite everyone back the next Friday. During the week, when you see people from the group around campus, make a point to stop and talk to them. Let them know that there are others on campus who care about them.

You have the power to combat loneliness on your campus. The question is: Are you going to use it?

Hanging Yourself Out to Dry

How to Ask Someone Out

Few things in life are as risky as asking someone for a first date. Talk about vulnerable! It's like handing the person a bag filled with your self-esteem, pride, and ego, and letting her decide whether or not she wants to dump it out all over the floor. To those of you with the guts to take this ultimate risk, we salute you—and offer you these tips.

Do Your Research

You spot her across the crowded dining hall. You've never seen her before, but you know you must see her again! You must ask her out, but she's walking up the stairs—and out of your life. Throwing caution to the wind, you make your way to her as quickly as you can, sliding past several large members of the football team in the process. You reach her just as she's walking out the door. "Hi," you say as smoothly as possible, "I saw you downstairs and I was wondering if you'd like to go to the football game with me Saturday." She doesn't answer right away, but instead looks over your right shoulder at the person standing behind you. "What do you think, Sweetie?" she asks, pointing at you. "Should I go out with him?" Just as you notice the engagement ring on her finger, you feel a hand the size of a dinner plate on your shoulder.

Save yourself some embarrassment—or worse. Get as much information as you can about a person before you ask her out. Find out what she's like, what she enjoys doing, and whether she has a significant other. You'll be glad you did.

Practice, Practice, Practice

A relaxed, confident attitude doesn't just come naturally, you know. Being suave and witty is hard work. It takes practice. You'll need to work on everything from your delivery to your smile to your posture. Get your hand motions down cold. Know exactly what you're going to say and do when you approach the person for a date. You want to be as relaxed as possible, so the more comfortable you are with your plan, the better you'll be.

PLAN FOR EVERYTHING

What's your next step if she says yes? How are you going to react if she says no? What will you do if she says no to this date, but then says she'd like to go out with you some other time? What happens if she can't answer you because she's laughing so hard? These are just four of the scenarios you'll need to plan for.

DO IT IN PERSON

A phone call may seem like a safer method if you're planning to get shot down in flames, but it's a poor substitute for a face-to-face encounter. For one thing, you can't read body language over the phone. You won't be able to tell if she raises her eyebrows in excitement or sticks her tongue out and makes gagging motions to her roommate. You also risk the embarrassment of having to explain who you are over the phone ("I have blond hair, blue eyes. . . . Yes, I'm the guy with the mole above my right eyebrow"). At least in person she can pretend she knows who you are.

DON'T MAKE A PRODUCTION OF IT

Sure, it would be really wacky if you draped a big sign in front of her dorm asking her out, but it might embarrass her. The last thing you want to do is embarrass a person you're asking out. A simple and sincere approach is the best. If you can do it in the middle of a casual conversation, all the better.

BE AS NONTHREATENING AS YOU POSSIBLY CAN

If the person you're hoping to date doesn't know you, the only thing she'll have to judge you by is the way you act when you're asking her out. So be on your best behavior. Communicate to her both verbally and nonverbally that you're someone she can trust. Don't invade her personal space while talking to her, and, for heaven's sake, do not touch her!

CATCH HER AT THE RIGHT TIME

They say timing is everything, and we believe them (whoever "they" are). So should you. Don't try to ask someone out while she's hurrying to get somewhere. You don't want her making a decision when she's stressed-out. *Here's another tip:* Don't ask someone out while she's sitting with a large group of friends. You don't want to put her on the spot, and you certainly don't want to hear snickers from the group when you ask. Try to catch her when she's alone or with a friend or two. Also try to catch her when she's feeling relaxed.

BE SPECIFIC

Don't say, "Would you like to go out sometime?" If she says no, it's a complete rejection of you and everything you stand for. She's saying, "No, I would never like to go out with you." Instead, be specific, giving her some leeway, should she decide to decline. Ask, "Would you like to go see the theater department's musical Friday night?" If she says no, you can either press her for details as to why (maybe she's busy Friday night; maybe she hates musicals) or you can cut your losses and walk away with at least a shred of dignity left, knowing that it may not have been you she rejected.

DON'T PLAN SOMETHING EXPENSIVE

Save the lobster dinners and limousine service for your second or third date. For your first one, do something inexpensive, casual, and interactive. If you do something too expensive on your first date, not only will you need to keep topping yourself, you may also be putting some pressure on your date to "live up" to the expense.

ACT LIKE YOU'VE DONE IT BEFORE

If she says yes, don't start running around the quad, high-fiving everyone you see. Don't start crying for joy. Don't fall to your knees whispering, "Thank you. Oh thank you!" If she says no, don't hang your head, kick at the dirt, and say, "I knew you wouldn't." Whether the answer's yes or no, carry yourself with dignity.

No Means No. . .Date for You

WHAT TO DO WHEN IT'S CLEAR YOU WON'T BE GOING OUT

No matter who you are or what you look like, if you ask enough girls out, sooner or later you are going to be rejected. Someone's going to knock you flat with a no. Sorry, it's the rules of the game. Nobody shoots 100 percent from the field in dating. Everyone gets shot down at least once. Believe it, accept it, deal with it, and plan for it.

Ouch!

"It's not the fact that she said no. It's the fact that every-one [else] heard it." —Comedian Robert Townsend in one of his routines

WOW!

Likewise, if you get asked for dates enough, sooner or later (but usually much, much sooner) you're going to say no. You're going to shoot some poor guy down, whether you realize it or not.

Recognizing these hard truths, we've put together a few guidelines for both men and women to assist you in handling and dealing with the Big No.

IF YOU'RE THE ASKER

If you've just been shot down after asking someone for a date, remember. . .

You can still salvage the situation and walk away with some self-respect.
If you prepare yourself for the possibility of rejection beforehand, you can turn a potentially uncomfortable situation into one that's just slightly awkward. Put a humorous spin on the rejection by saying something like, "I respect your choice, but I think I should warn you that most of the guys around here go for ugly girls, so it may be awhile before you get another date offer." It's a pretty classy move to compliment a young woman and make her laugh after she's rejected you. She'll respect you for it (whether she tells you so or not).

It's not necessarily a reflection on you.

Don't think of yourself as a reject just because one person rejected you. If you don't know the young woman's circumstances, don't assume she declined your date invitation because she didn't like you. Maybe she's already dating someone. Maybe she's just been dumped and isn't ready to start dating again. Maybe she's ashamed of some personal habit and prefers not to get close to people.

Even if she says to you, "Get away from me, you ugly creep, and don't ever think about talking to me again," don't take it too hard. There are plenty of people who would love to be asked out by you. Find them.

Learn from your mistakes.

Did you mistime your approach? Maybe you caught her at a bad time. Maybe she was late for a class. Maybe she'd just gotten into a fight with her roommate. Maybe she was worried about an upcoming test. Maybe she'd just awakened from a nap and was still a little grouchy. In short, maybe *circumstances* were what killed your chance for a date.

Were you intense and scary? Did you invade her personal space? Did you come off like a stalker? Did your nervousness get the better of you? How tense did the scene get? Did she breathe a sigh of relief when you walked away? If so, you're going to have to ratchet down that intensity level next time.

Did you have something disgusting hanging from your nose? Unless you want to be known as Booger Boy, always check the mirror and give yourself a swipe or two before moving in for the kill. The last thing you need are a couple of nasal refugees blowing your first impression on a young lady. Review your work. Take notes, if you must. Rethink your strategy. Polish your approach. Don't make the same mistakes again.

If You're the Askee

If you've just shot someone down after getting asked for a date, remember. . .

Don't apologize.

You have no reason to be sorry. You did nothing but tell the truth to someone who asked you a question. Besides, what is it exactly that you're apologizing for?

- "I'm sorry I don't find you interesting or attractive enough to spend a few hours with."
- "I'm sorry I had to knock your self-confidence level down a few notches."
- "I'm sorry you put me in the awkward position of having to shoot you down."
- "I'm sorry I gave you any reason to believe that I would be attracted to someone like you."

You may think you're being sweet to the guy and letting him off easy, but an apology will sound like condescension to anyone who receives it.

Don't unwittingly lead the other person on.
Be direct in your response: "No, I am not interested in going on a date with you." It may seem unnecessarily harsh to you, but the more direct you are, the better it will be for the guy in the long run.

What you want to avoid is giving the guy a reason to think that if he asks you out later, he'll get a different answer. Don't say you have plans with your roommate or that your parents are in town. Tell it like it is. You'll save everyone involved a lot of time and grief.

Have a heart.
Be direct and clear, but don't be cruel (sorry, Elvis). A good rule of thumb here is that the less you laugh at and make fun of the guy who asks you out, the better he'll take the rejection. All you really need to do is put yourself in the guy's position and think about how you'd prefer to be rejected.

Important tip: Please don't ever use the old "I like you as a friend" line. You may think you're complimenting the guy on how much his friendship means to you. He won't take it that way. Imagine how you'd feel if your date told you that you remind him of his mother? That's what the "let's just be friends" line feels like to a guy.

At the risk of ending this section on a somber note, we would like to remind you that if you encounter a guy who will not take no for an answer, someone who continues to contact you after you've asked him not to, you should contact campus police. The earlier someone intervenes in a potential stalking case, the better.

BREAKUPS MADE EASIER

Unless you marry the person you're dating now, there's a very good chance that the two of you will break up. When it comes to that point, will you know what to do and say? Here are some tips for you.

Tip #1: Don't Draw It Out Any More Than You Have To.

If you think your breakup is going to occur in one specific place at one specific time, you're being a little naive. Most breakups occur over the course of five to seven separate meetings, not unlike a World Series. The first meeting is the dropping of the bomb. Usually not much is said on this night because the dumpee (our shorthand term for the person on the receiving end of the breakup) is stunned into silence. When the dumpee recovers slightly—usually the next morning—meeting number two begins. This is usually a rehash of the first meeting, with the dumpee asking questions here and there. The third meeting occurs when the dumpee gets angry about the breakup. This is the place where harsh words are often exchanged. The fourth meeting is then initiated by an apology for the harsh words of the third meeting. By the fifth meeting, reality—and usually depression—has set in. The dumpee traditionally initiates this meeting as a way of letting the dumper know how depressed he or she is. Meetings six and seven usually involve the dumper checking on the well-being of the dumpee.

The longer the breakup process drags on, the longer it is before healing can begin. The best thing you, the dumper, can do is not to keep rehashing the breakup over and over with your "ex." Firmly (but gently) refuse to meet with your ex after everything has been said. Don't keep reopening the breakup wounds.

Tip #2: Don't Do It at a Really Bad Time.

If the person you're dating is facing a crisis, whether it's a critically ill relative or a personal medical emergency, you may want to think twice about breaking up right away. It may seem unfair for you to have to endure a relationship you want out of, but it's even more unfair to add to your boyfriend's or girlfriend's emotional turmoil. Save the breakup news until the person is strong enough to receive it.

Tip #3: Don't Let It Come as a Total Surprise.

Do something to get the message across. Breaking up with someone without any advance warning is just plain cruel. If your date thinks the relationship is going great and getting deeper each day, the bomb you drop will feel more explosive. If there's a way you two are incompatible, point it out as it comes. Don't surprise the other person with something you've been living with for some time.

Pressure Cooker

WOW!

"You know, I'm gonna be the best husband, the best father, the best lover. But how am I supposed to convey that over a cheap salad and a bowl of cold soup?"
—An anonymous junior commenting on a dining-hall date in *The Wheaton Record*, the newspaper of Wheaton College.

Tip #4: Don't Be Cruel.

If you've been hurt in the relationship, your first instinct will be to hurt the other person more. Don't follow that instinct. Assuming that this is the last time the two of you will be together, there's no reason you can't remain civil long enough to talk about the reasons for the breakup. Don't let anger and cruelty worm their way into the discussion.

Tip #5: Don't Do It Out of Anger.

If your breakup is the result of a big, angry fight, it's a bad breakup. You're going to have to do it again. So many things are said in anger in the heat of battle that it's hard to figure out what's from the heart and what's said for effect. After you've cooled down from the fight, talk about the real reasons the two of you should break up.

Tip #6: Don't Focus on the Negative.

Don't talk about all the things that were wrong with the relationship—that is, unless the dumpee asks you to. Instead, focus on the fact that you don't believe the two of you are right for each other. Don't let the person think, *If only I'd done this differently, we'd still be together.* Help him or her see that the breakup was not caused by one or two specific instances, but by two different, and ultimately incompatible, people.

Tip #7: Don't Say, "Can We Still Be Friends?"

There's nothing wrong with remaining friends after a breakup. We just can't stand that old line. If you could come up with something fresher or more original, we would appreciate it. The truth is, few people manage to be friends after a breakup—at least for some time. The deeper the emotions are involved, the longer it may be before you can be "friends" again.

Section 9
Campus Life

Just Be Smart

HARMFUL SUBSTANCES ON CAMPUS

A world of opportunities awaits you in college. Unfortunately, not all of those opportunities are good. On campus, you're going to be confronted with many lifestyle choices. Some of these choices will involve illegal or harmful substances. You're going to need to make some decisions on how you plan to avoid destroying your health with alcohol, drugs, and tobacco.

ALCOHOL

Alcohol has long been the drug of choice among college students in the United States. According to the Center for Substance Abuse Prevention, college students spend approximately $4.2 billion annually on alcohol. In one year, college students purchase over four billion cans of beer. And the problem is growing.

The presidents of several major universities around the country identified *binge drinking* as the most serious problem on campus today. For men, binge drinking means downing at least five alcoholic drinks in a row; for women, it's four alcoholic drinks in a row. Binge drinking is not social drinking, a means for feeling comfortable in a crowd. Bingeing is purposefully drinking oneself into oblivion.

Harvard University's School of Public Health surveyed students at 140 colleges and found that:

- 44 percent of the students had engaged in binge drinking during the two weeks before the survey.

- 50 percent of the men reported having five or more drinks in a row.

- 39 percent of the women reported having four or more drinks in a row.

- Binge drinkers in high school are three times more likely to binge in college.

- The percentage of students who were binge drinkers was nearly uniform from freshman to senior year, despite the fact that the legal age for drinking is 21.

- 20 percent of the students were *frequent* binge drinkers, meaning they binged *three or more times* in a two-week period!

The students reported several different reasons for their drinking habits, including the status associated with drinking, the overall culture of drinking on campus, peer pressure, and academic stress.

You probably wouldn't be surprised to know that drinkers are more likely than nondrinkers to miss class, fall behind in schoolwork, engage in unplanned sexual activity, get in trouble with campus police, and use other drugs. What you may not know is how other people are affected by drinking. The Harvard survey showed:

- 67 percent of the students surveyed reported experiencing at least one adverse consequence from another student's drinking.

- 44 percent had to "baby-sit" an intoxicated student.

- 43 percent had their sleep or study interrupted.

- 27 percent had been insulted or humiliated.

- 22 percent had a serious argument.

- 21 percent had an unwanted sexual advance.

- 13 percent had been assaulted.

- 12 percent suffered property damage.

- 2 percent had been the victim of date rape or sexual assault.

These numbers suggest that even if you choose not to drink in college—a very wise choice, by the way—you will be affected by someone who does drink.

If you'd like a few more deterrents to drinking, we've got them for you. Student drinking is the number one health problem on university campuses today. Researchers say that alcohol is a factor in about 41 percent of all academic problems. Ninety percent of all rapes occur while either the victim or attacker is under the influence of alcohol. What's more, alcohol has been closely linked to criminal activity, vandalism, the spread of sexually transmitted diseases, car accidents, drownings, and suicides.

Need we say more?

The concerns about college drinking aren't just coming from worried parents anymore. They're coming from all sectors of society—from government health officials to fraternity and sorority leaders. Maybe you don't understand how serious the problem is. If that's the case, please take our word for it. Stay away from alcohol while you're in school.

In addition to these concerns, there are legal reasons, too. Drinking under the legal age could have its own consequences. While it seems a minor infraction to some people, any intentional lawbreaking disappoints God, who expects Christians to obey the government.

DRUGS

College is the ideal breeding ground for drug use. Think about it. One of the major reasons for attending college is to expand one's mind. That's the same reason many people use to explain their drug use. College students, out from under their parents' influence, are likely to question their old

Get Help!

If you suspect that you or someone you know has a drug problem, you must **DON'T FORGET** act *immediately*. The problem will only get worse. Contact your school health provider, a local community hot line, a local Narcotics Anonymous program, or the National Institute Drug Abuse Hotline at 1-800-662-HELP.

value system—a value system that told them drugs were wrong. On campus, students are going to meet a wide range of personality types, some of whom may defy their previous notions about what a drug user is like. Seeing "normal people" use drugs may change their attitudes toward controlled substances. Finally, on a college campus, students are simply going to have more exposure to drugs and more opportunities to try them.

That's a problem, you see, because the pressures, loneliness, and insecurity that go along with the college experience creates a breeding ground for drug abuse and addiction. Once a student finds a way to ease the pressure, dull the loneliness, or escape the insecurity through drugs, the temptation will be there to return again and again to that escape route. Would it sound too simplistic and naive to suggest that the best way to prevent developing a drug habit is to never do drugs in the first place? If so, forget that we suggested it.

According to the Center for Substance Abuse Prevention, almost one-third of all college students used marijuana in the past year. For you nonmath majors, that's one in three. So if you're sitting next to two people in class, statistics suggest that one of you has been smoking joints recently. The statistics for hard drugs go like this: 5.6 percent of all college students have used cocaine in the past year, 4.3 percent have used LSD, and a combined 3.3 percent have used heroin or other opiates.

If you come from a high school where drug use was rampant, these statistics may not mean much to you. For you, the adjustment to college will not be as difficult as it will be for others. If, on the other hand, you come from a high school where drug use was not widespread, you may be looking at some serious adjustments when you get to college. If you've been sheltered from drug use your entire life (a prospect that's becoming less and less likely in today's society), an eye-opening experience awaits you at college.

Don't think that if you're going to a Christian college, you'll be immune from the problem. Though the numbers aren't nearly as high as they are on secular campuses, drugs are a problem everywhere. Let's put it this way: At some point during your college career, you will be exposed to drug use—and possibly drug *abuse*—in one form or another. And you need to be prepared.

Would you be able to recognize symptoms of drug abuse if you saw it in, say, your roommate? Here are some warning signs to look for:

- A generally unhealthy lifestyle
- Poor personal health
- Noticeable weight loss
- Inconsistent class attendance
- Mood swings that go from giddiness to depression
- Regular anxiety and nervousness
- Undependability and trouble handling responsibilities
- Financial problems or always being strapped for cash

Most drug abusers believe they can stop taking drugs at any time. They're wrong. What's more, their denial could result in rejection by family and friends, legal or financial trouble, overdose, and possibly death.

TOBACCO

Many people who never would have considered smoking before take up the habit in college to help them deal with the pressures of studying and socializing. The decision may seem harmless enough on the surface. After all, what's the big deal with a cigarette now and then?

Okay, let's run through some of the facts. Smoking is an addiction. Tobacco contains nicotine, a drug that is extremely addictive. Once you start smoking for any length of time, it is very difficult to quit.

CATCH A CLUE

Quit Today!

If you would like more information about kicking the habit, call 1-800-4-CANCER.

Do you want some statistics and medical findings? Try these. Smoking is responsible for about 30 percent of all cancer deaths in the United States annually. Smoking increases the risk of heart attack and stroke. It has been linked to osteoporosis, a bone-thinning disease that affects as many as twenty-five to thirty million people in this country, killing over a million people every year.

Studies show that about half of the smokers who began smoking when they were teenagers will eventually die from it, probably prematurely in middle age, cutting twenty to twenty-five years from their life expectancies.

Of course, you're too old to fall for the old line that smoking is cool. As a mature college student, you're certainly not going to start sucking on "cancer sticks" because of what you think it will do for your image. Right? You do know that "Smoking is cool" is one of the most laughably absurd myths ever to make the rounds of high schools and junior highs across the nation. Surely if you were going to choose a reason to smoke, it wouldn't be "coolness."

But here are some other myths about smoking that you may not be so clear on.

• Only heavy smoking is fatal.

• If you've smoked for many years, stopping will have little effect.

• Smoking only kills people in old age.

Wrong, wrong, and wrong. Approximately 30 percent of all eighteen to twenty-five year olds in the United States smoke. If you're one of them, or if you're thinking about becoming one of them, here are some reasons to stop (or not to start).

• You will be able to taste and smell food better.

• Your breath will smell better.

• Your cough will go away.

• You will save a surprising amount of money.

• You will protect your friends and family members from second-hand smoke, a very serious health risk.

• You will greatly reduce your risk of lung cancer (and other forms of cancer), heart disease, stroke, lung diseases, or other respiratory illnesses.

Whatever satisfaction comes from alcohol, drugs, and smoking is temporary at best. Do not allow these substances to spoil your college years or ruin your life.

It's All Greek to Me

Have you considered the Greek question yet? Will you be pledging a fraternity or sorority? Do you know enough about the Greek system to make an informed decision? Here's a brief rundown of some of the pros and cons of fraternities and sororities that you may want to take into consideration before you decide anything.

THE CASE FOR FRATERNITIES AND SORORITIES

One of the strongest arguments for joining a fraternity or sorority is precedence. The fact is, *many* Christian young people have pledged themselves to the Greek system and lived to tell about it. These believers have been able to maintain their own standards and beliefs within the system and serve as Christian witnesses to their fellow members. They point out that Christians have been sent to all corners of the globe—including the Greek corner—to proclaim the gospel. They see a need for Christians to be represented in all areas of college life. What's more, many of them see no serious conflict between their Christian values and the stated goals of the fraternity or sorority.

From a practical standpoint, fraternities and sororities offer an automatic "in" to the college community. What's more, most fraternities and sororities are involved in the community, both on campus and in surrounding areas. They do valuable work to raise money for worthy causes. They promote political agendas and sponsor campus issues they believe in. And by setting a required minimum grade point average for their members, it could be argued that fraternities and sororities are encouraging academic excellence.

Here are three good reasons to consider going Greek.

• It can be a great networking experience for jobs.

• It teaches the responsibility of taking care of a house.

• On some campuses, it's the only social scene around.

Furthermore, supporters of the Greek system point out that it is unfair to make categorically negative statements about fraternities and sororities. With the good comes the bad, they argue. You cannot judge one school's Greek system based on the exploits and notoriety of another school's system. They point out that not all Greek systems are exclusionary; some are open to anyone who would like to join. In short, they say don't automatically deem the Greek system inappropriate for Christian students.

THE CASE AGAINST FRATERNITIES AND SORORITIES

You've probably guessed that there are some aspects of fraternities and sororities that do not necessarily lend themselves to spiritual enrichment. There are some reasons that thoughtful, concerned Christian students may want to think twice before pledging Greek.

Alcohol

The first and most glaring reason may be boiled down to seven little letters: A-L-C-O-H-O-L. Behind the civic-mindedness that most fraternities and sororities are involved with is one nonstop keg party. (Okay, this is more true for fraternities than sororities, but the point is still valid.) Life often revolves around drinking. In fact, the Greek system has been blamed for creating and fostering the biggest problem on college campuses today: binge drinking. Fraternities have become training grounds of sorts for future alcoholics. One of the first questions you'll need to ask yourself is how you feel about drunkenness, drugs, sex, and other debauchery, because those can pretty much describe the weekend agendas of many college fraternities and sororities.

CATCH A CLUE

Decide Yourself

The worst thing you could do is make a decision on fraternities and sororities based on what you've heard or suspect to be true. Find out for yourself what the Greek system on your campus is like. Talk to people in the system as well as people who have chosen not to join. On the other hand, do not allow social pressures to force you into a system you're uncomfortable with. Your choice to join or not to join a fraternity or sorority should be made only after personal investigation and no small amount of prayer.

Snob Factor

Often students are invited to join a fraternity or sorority based on their looks, their athletic ability, their personal wealth, and their family ties to the organization. Some Greek systems have been accused of racism and discrimination. If you thought social pecking orders were a high school phenomenon, think again.

Hell Week

You've probably seen or read news reports of underclassmen being killed as a result of a hazing incident gone wrong. *Hazing* refers to the initiations most pledges must undergo in order to join a fraternity or sorority. Most hazing occurs during what's known as "hell week." The majority of the initiations are humiliating and stupid. Some are extremely dangerous, even life threatening. Fraternities and sororities argue that these initiations strengthen a pledge's loyalty and bond to the group.

Time

Finally, living in a large house like this can actually take a lot of *time*. There are house meetings, chores, and other obligations that will be expected of you.

Alive and Well on Campus

PERSONAL SAFETY TIPS FOR COLLEGE LIFE

Most colleges and universities go to great lengths to ensure the safety of their students. Yet even the comprehensive measures taken by the schools cannot match the effectiveness of personal precaution when it comes to safety. In the next few pages you'll find important information about personal safety and crime prevention. Take this information to heart. It may be all that stands between you and a potential crime.

THE MOST COMMON CAMPUS CRIMES AND WHAT YOU CAN DO TO PREVENT THEM

Call them the "big three," the most frequently occurring crimes on college campuses. Theft, burglary, and physical assaults have become part of the fabric of college life. But that doesn't mean they're inevitable. You can do quite a bit to prevent yourself from becoming a victim. Here are just some of the precautions you can take.

Theft

Theft tops the list as the most commonly reported crime on college campuses. Among the items favored by thieves are bicycles, backpacks, purses, and wallets. The good news is that by following a few simple guidelines, you can make a thief's job extremely difficult. Lock your bike any time you leave it in an area with heavy foot traffic. If possible, use a krypton-type lock. When you set down a purse or backpack, keep it in your peripheral vision at all times. And never leave your belongings unattended.

Burglary

Incidents of people breaking into an apartment or dorm room to steal property is less common than straight theft. Still, burglary accounts for a significant percentage of the crimes that occur on college campuses. One of the most effective ways for preventing burglary is to keep the door to your apartment or dorm room locked at all times. Dead bolts and other such safety-lock devices provide added protection and are highly recommended. Under no circumstances should you ever let strangers into your home. Do not leave spare keys under your doormat or in other obvious hiding places. For the sake of identification, inscribe all items of value with your driver's license number.

Assault

Physical assault, instances of people causing bodily injury to someone else, is the least reported of the so-called "common" campus crimes. However, it must be pointed out that statistics on sexual assault, including rape, date rape, or acquaintance rape, are hard to quantify since so many of these crimes go unreported. It's safe to say that sexual assault occurs much more frequently than police reports indicate. Because of the growing number of problems associated with this crime on campus, we're devoting the next section to a discussion of sexual assault.

WHAT ARE SEX CRIMES?

There are, disturbingly, more types of sex crimes than we could list here. For our purposes, we will limit our discussion to three of the most commonly occurring types on college campuses.

Sexual Assault

Sexual assault is defined as any sexual activity forced upon one person by another. And while that may be clear from a legal sense, for many people the line is not so obviously drawn. Many victims fail to report sexual assault simply because they are not absolutely sure that an assault has taken place. Other victims may suspect that they are somehow responsible for the attack, believing that they did something to encourage it or didn't do enough to prevent it. Let's be clear here: "No" means no. If, after you've indicated that you are not willing to have sex, the assailant does not stop, then sexual assault has occurred.

Sexual Harassment

The difference between sexual harassment and sexual assault is that in a harassment case no one is physically abused. That does not mean, however, that a crime has not taken place. Examples of harassment may include repeated and unwanted romantic advances, sexually explicit discussions, abusive language aimed at a particular sex, lewd jokes, and unwanted touching. Do not assume that you're being a prude for not "playing along" with sexual harassment. You do not need to put up with anything that makes you uncomfortable.

Date Rape or Acquaintance Rape

Pay careful attention to this statistic: The *overwhelming* majority of rapes on campus are committed by someone the victim knows. It is foolish and dangerous to assume that you're "safe" with someone you know. Furthermore, it is absolutely wrong to assume that an assault is ever the victim's fault. While the victim may regret being in the position that led to the assault, the crime should never be blamed on the victim. The assault occurs *against* the victim, never *because* of that victim.

How Can Sex Crimes Be Prevented?

A young person on a college campus can go a long way toward protecting against sexual assault simply by incorporating a few preventative measures.

In a Dating Situation

Clearly communicate to your date what you want and don't want. Set your physical limits before you actually go out. Make sure you're on the same page so that you both know what to expect on the date. While you're on the date, be aware of any mixed signals you may be sending.

These are good ideas for preventing sexual assault. There are, however, two *great* ideas for protecting yourself from rape: Do not drink and do not hang around with people who are drinking. Research indicates that up to *90 percent* of all sexual assaults on campus involve alcohol. Common sense says that if you remove alcohol from the equation, you lessen the possibility of sexual assault significantly.

In a Dangerous Situation

If you find yourself in a situation where there is a potential for sexual assault, there are several tactics you can use to put off your attacker. The first tactic is to name the offense. Tell your attacker that a sexual assault is being committed (or sexual harassment). Sometimes this serves as a slap in the face or a wake-up call to the would-be attacker and stops the event. Sometimes, though, it puts the attacker off only for a moment.

If the situation becomes more dire, your actions should become more forceful. If the assailant continues to advance on you, scream to draw attention to yourself. Yell "No!" "Stop!" "Help!" or anything that will get the attention of others. If you can, run away. Remove yourself from the situation. If that's not possible, and if worse comes to worst, fight back against your attacker using any means or objects at your disposal.

This is important: If you have any questions about sexual assault or if you think you may be the victim of an assault or harassment, talk to a counselor who deals with such cases. Your campus medical facility or local hospital has trained professionals on staff who can help you understand what has happened. Whether you report sexual assault to the police or not, we urge you to seek immediate medical treatment. Do not shower, change clothes, or do anything else that might destroy evidence before you see a doctor.

THE BOTTOM LINE

Fundamental Safety Tips for College Students

Get to know the routes you'll be taking to and from your classes, job, and residence hall each day. Find out where the nearest emergency phones are located on those routes.

Give your parents and a small circle of close friends a copy of your schedule, so that they will know where you are supposed to be at any given time. Give a "network" list of phone numbers to your parents, your academic advisor, and your friends.

Never walk alone after daylight hours. Never take "shortcuts" from your regular (presumably safe) routes. Always travel in groups or use a shuttle service after dark.

Never loan your keys to anyone for any purpose. If you or your roommate loses a key, request an immediate lock change.

Always lock your windows and doors at night. Never compromise your safety for the sake of a roommate who wants to sneak back in sometime during the night.

Never leave valuables like identification, wallets, checkbooks, jewelry, cameras, or anything else in open view in your room.

Program your phone's speed-dial memory with emergency numbers that include family and friends.

Get to know your neighbors. Don't be reluctant to report illegal activities or suspicious loitering around the building.

Our final piece of advice for keeping yourself safe on campus is to trust your instincts. Keep your eyes and ears open at all times. If something doesn't feel right, whether it's a person, place, or situation, get away from it.

A Little Friendly Competition

INTRAMURALS

On some college campuses, varsity games are the second-biggest sporting events on campus. The real competitive excitement can be found on the campus intramural courts and fields. Whether it's basketball, flag football, soccer, softball, or coed volleyball, you can usually find an intramural game being played somewhere on campus. Let's take a look at the phenomenon known as intramurals.

WHAT ARE INTRAMURALS ALL ABOUT?

Depending on who you listen to, intramurals serve any number of purposes on the college campus. For one thing, they give high school athletes—those who were unable or unwilling to play interschool sports—a chance to polish their games and compete in the activities they enjoy most. And what competition it is! The competitiveness and skills demonstrated in high-level intramural games often exceed those found in interschool sports. Some people, in fact, use intramurals to improve their games enough to make varsity teams. Others use intramural contests to showcase their skills for the coaches and scouts who often attend the games. If you're not skilled enough to compete at this level, it's still fun to watch these intramural games.

Even for those not looking to further their athletic careers, intramurals can be a great source of competition and exercise. Intramural leagues are usually divided into levels, based on players' skills. If you find the level that's right for you, you can guarantee yourself a heaping helping of competition. If you enjoy competing, you'll thrive in an intramural environment.

For some people, competition is a secondary benefit of intramurals. Their primary motivation is energy release. After sitting through lectures and studying all day, they've got pent-up energy that they need to get rid of. And what better place to release it than a sporting activity? So intramurals are like a reward for the hardworking student.

Intramurals are also a great opportunity for fellowship. First, there's the bond that's developed among teammates. If you're looking to make friends on campus, one of your best bets is to sign up for your floor's intramural teams. Aside from getting to know the people on your team, you'll also have an opportunity to meet people from around the campus when you compete against them. Many solid college friendships are built from intramural competition.

WHAT YOU SHOULD KNOW ABOUT INTRAMURALS

The first thing you should know about intramural sports is that there are a lot of great athletes playing them. Were you a good athlete in high school—maybe the best basketball player on the team, the highest scorer in soccer, the leading receiver in football? You're about to find out that there are dozens and dozens of people every bit as good as you are playing intramural sports. If you used to be a big fish in a small pond, welcome to the ocean. As we mentioned earlier, most intramural leagues are separated into three or four divisions (*A, B, C,* and sometimes *D*), according to the players' skill level.

WOW!

Turning Pro
Believe it or not, you can make some money from intramural sports on campus. No, we're not talking about getting paid to play. And we're certainly not talking about betting on games. We're talking about getting involved as an intramural coordinator.

People are needed to schedule the games, coordinate the use of the necessary facilities, check the rosters, post the standings, keep the statistics, monitor the games, work as umpires or referees, and address rules infractions. Many of these are paid positions. And if there's anything better than being involved in intramural athletics on campus, it's getting paid for the privilege.

A level is for the cream of the athletic crop. These are people who have both the size and skills to play. Many *A*-level players could play varsity ball on some college teams.

B level is for people who have the skills to play at the top level, but not the size—and sometimes for people who have the size, but not the skills. This is where a lot of good high school players choose to compete.

C level is for people who are mostly interested in having fun. They may know the game, but they don't have the skills necessary to play it well or are more interested in having a good time than in winning.

D level usually exists only on very large campuses. *D*-level players are usually just looking to kill an hour or two doing something that vaguely resembles a sport.

I Can't Get around How You Get Around

TRANSPORTATION ON CAMPUS

For the purposes of this book, we're going to narrow your on-campus transportation options to three: biking, driving, or walking. (You roller bladers are on your own.)

BIKING

Some colleges do not allow first-semester freshmen to bring cars to campus. So for at least four months, students are presented with the choice of walking or riding a bike when they need to get somewhere. (A third option is bumming a ride from someone else, but that will get tiring very quickly—not necessarily for you, but for the people you leech from.)

How would you feel about tooling around campus on two wheels? Many college students swear by their bikes. They point out that biking gives them more exercise than driving but isn't as slow as walking. Most campuses are well equipped with bike racks in front of most of buildings and bike paths throughout the campus.

Should you decide that biking is your best transportation bet, you'll next need to decide what kind of bike to get. Bicycles can run from a couple hundred to several thousand dollars. The question is, what will you be using your bike for? If it's to schlep around campus, all you'll need is an inexpensive, yet fairly dependable, pair of wheels and a frame. If you're looking to become a serious cyclist in your free time, you may want to opt for a more expensive racing bike. If you're planning on some two-wheel, off-road action, try out some mountain bikes. If you're looking to pick up dates while you ride, look at some two seaters.

If you choose a bike as your primary mode of transportation, keep this in mind: Bicycles are among the most often stolen items on college campuses. Keep your eyes on your wheels. Always lock your bike in a place where there's heavy foot traffic. Always use a krypton-type lock. Furthermore, when you're riding, stay away from desolate paths and wooded areas. Whenever possible, ride with someone else.

DRIVING

Will it be worth it to you to have a car on campus? Let's consider some of the pros and cons. The pros include instant access to transportation, regardless of weather or time of day; a place for your date to ride when you go out; and the freedom to go home or anywhere else you'd like to go whenever you want. The cons include the expenses of gas, oil changes, major repairs, registration, insurance, and so on. You'll need to ask yourself not only whether you have the money to buy a car, but also the money to maintain a car.

If you decide to buy a car for use on campus, what should you look for? Do you want something that will get you noticed and admired? Or will any dependable vehicle fit the bill? Do you want an ocean liner, something big enough to transport half your floor to the local pizza place? (If so, don't allow yourself to get roped into being your friends' chauffeur—that is, unless they're good about kicking in dough for gas and mileage.) Or will a little telephone booth on wheels suit your transportation needs?

If you have a car on campus, there are some safety issues you'll need to think about.

- Make sure that you always park in well-lighted areas close to where people walk. Never sacrifice safety for convenience. Don't park in an unsafe area even if it means you're closer to where you need to be.

- Lock all doors and roll up all windows when you get out of your car. Lock the doors again when you get back in the car; leave your windows up until you're safely moving.
- Never leave valuables in plain sight in your car. You might as well leave a note on your window that says, "To get to my wallet, simply smash this window."
- Hold your keys in your hand when you're returning to your vehicle at night to allow yourself quick entry. Whenever possible, walk with someone you know and trust on your way back to your car at night.
- Never pick up or give a ride to anyone you don't know. That includes everyone from the nice guy who works in the bookstore to the new person your roommate is seeing.
- If you are carjacked—that is, if someone gets into your car while you're in it and demands that you relinquish it—surrender your vehicle immediately. It's better to let the police track the car down than to risk your life trying to argue with a felon.

WALKING

Some people prefer the most primitive method of transportation available, and why not? Walking will provide you with the best workout possible. Unfortunately, though, exercise is not the only consideration when it comes to walking. You're also going to have to consider the geographical region you're living in. If you're attending the University of Minnesota, how many months out of the year will you be able to walk around campus? You'll also need to consider how walking-friendly your college is. Are the campus buildings spread out miles apart? Are they located in less-than-safe neighborhoods? Are the grounds sufficiently lighted and patrolled? Finally, you'll need to consider your footwear. Do you have the shoes to accommodate a great deal of walking? Will you carry an extra pair to wear in class? Are you sufficiently equipped to be a campus walker?

If you decide that walking is the means of transportation for you, you're going to have to take measures to keep yourself safe at all times. The first and most obvious suggestion is to avoid, whenever possible, walking alone or with someone you don't know. Next, you'll want to get to know the routes you'll be taking to and from your classes, your job, your residence hall, and anywhere else you go regularly. Make sure you know where the nearest emergency phones are located along those routes. Never take "shortcuts" from your regular routes, no matter how much time you'll save. After dark, always travel in groups or use a shuttle service.

Section 10
Leaving School

Postgrad Plans

PLAN AHEAD

Surely you've imagined what life after college will be like. (Being involved in a fabulous career? Finally going out on the mission field? Going into active military service? Going off to grad school?) The wise person plans ahead, rather than waiting and panicking. There are steps you

Questions to Consider

What career(s) are you considering? Why? What steps will you take now to plan your future? What steps have you already taken?

CATCH A CLUE

can take today—before you leave school—to prepare for tomorrow. If your very first step is prayer, then you're on a wise course. After all, "a man's steps are directed by the LORD" (Proverbs 20:24); "He guides the humble in what is right and teaches them His way" (Psalm 25:9). (Also Psalms 23:3; 25:5; 43:3.)

First year

If you're a freshman now, you're probably just considering your options for majors. Talk to professors within the programs you're thinking about. Ask about the career options for such majors. Then try to find a summer job in your chosen career or a career you're just considering for now. Want to go into photography? Work in a photo lab. Church ministry? Help out in a church office—the hub of many churches.

Second year

Narrow your focus. Once you've decided on a major (one that will move you in your chosen path), consider whether or not you'll need to go to grad school to fulfill your career choices. Talk to people with jobs in your chosen field. You can also meet with a counselor at the placement office for guidance. Look for a summer job in your chosen career.

Third year

Your junior year is the time to sign up for internships. Internships look great on a résumé. Speaking of résumés, start writing yours. This is also the time to begin researching grad schools.

Fourth year

As a senior, you'll take grad-school exams and send out applications. If you're looking to get into the workforce right away, you'll need to develop a list of potential employers. Take advantage of on-campus job fairs, campus visits by recruiters, and job-opportunity postings.

WRITING A RÉSUMÉ

The résumé in short. A résumé offers you the chance to put your best foot forward. After all, this is an employer's first view of you (after your cover letter of course). Use one sheet—8½ x 11—for your résumé. Include the facts about your life that make you shine. Employers will be most interested in your education, any work experience you have gained, and your skills. List both your schooling and your work experience in reverse chronological order. Work experience includes internships, part-time jobs, and volunteer jobs. Don't worry if you haven't had a "glamorous" internship or summer job. Any position of responsibility you have had could be useful. If, however, you were fired from a job or quit after a few weeks, *do not* list that position. Also, do not *lie* if *asked* about unsuccessful jobs you have held.

Some students include their GPAs on their résumé. Include yours only if the information will help you. If your GPA is 1.67, leaving it off is in your best interest! If the words *summa cum laude, magna cum laude,* or *cum laude* come with your degree, include them. You can also include your special achievements and extracurricular activities. Why? Because they show your interests and well roundedness. Did you receive a scholarship to attend college? Include that on your résumé. Are you currently on the student council? Jot that down! If the achievement is special to you, list it. But don't list that you just received your first hole in one or finally had that troublesome wisdom tooth taken out!

To Include or Not to Include an Objective

An objective is a statement about the type of job for which you are looking. Is an objective necessary on a résumé? Not necessarily. If you have a lot of work experience, you may need the space. If you do include an objective, you don't have to use the same one over and over for every résumé you send out. You might change your objective based on different types of jobs that interest you.

References.

Include on your résumé the phrase *References available on request.* References are those people in your life who can give a good report about you. References are usually people not related to you. Did you work on campus for the same professor for four years? He or she is a good reference. List the people who know you well. Although references don't have to be listed on the résumé, you should keep a list of possible references in case you're asked about them. On your reference list, include each person's name, address, phone number, work title, and relationship to you. (For example, Sarah Anne Linz, 1445 Spellman Road, 555-1212, Senior Editor, my internship supervisor.)

When you write your résumé, you can keep it on file at the placement office of your college. The placement office can send your résumé to employers (if requested). See the sample résumé for ideas.

COVER LETTERS

What is a cover letter? It is a letter that accompanies a résumé. Why use one? A cover letter provides a way to be professionally courteous and to let the recipient know why you are sending a résumé. A cover letter is usually brief—about one page. Include the recipient's name, work title, and work address. While you don't have to list what's on your résumé, you do need to communicate who you are, the type of position you're looking for, the person or source who referred you (a professor, an ad in the Sunday paper), and a brief description of your education ("I am currently a junior at Brown University"; "I recently received a B.S. in computer science"; "I am the editor of my college newspaper.") Always include a cover letter when you send out a résumé. A computer will allow you to use macros as you craft your cover letters. *Do not* photocopy a cover letter to send to multiple employers. Each recipient should receive an original.

Evelyn Jelicol

Objective

To help promote Heavenly Pizza's products and gain an entry-level position in marketing.

Education

1995–1998   Messiah College   Grantham, PA
• B.A., Business Administration and Marketing. GPA 3.5.

Experience

1998–1999   AF&F Phone Company   Philadelphia, PA
Marketing Internship
• Wrote first draft of letters for mass mailings.
• Developed plan for an antislamming advertising campaign.
• Worked in phone bank making telemarketing calls.
• Worked on task force that created the successful marketing campaign: "Call your mother. It's only a dime."

1997   The College Reader   Grantham, PA
Advertising Editor
• Called area businesses to secure advertising.
• Created page layouts for full-page advertisements.
• Increased revenue for paper by 35 percent.
• Increased distribution 15 percent.

Other information

• Skilled in the following software programs: Microsoft Word, Excel, Quark Xpress, and PageMaker.

PHONE (123) 098-7654 • EMAIL ME@ISP.COM
12345 GRACE STREET • FAIR LAWN, NJ 12345

Sample Résumé

THE CAREER SERVICES/JOB PLACEMENT OFFICE. . .AND YOU

This office may have different titles at different schools, but its purpose is the same—to help students find jobs. Go here for:

- Internships
- Summer, part-time, and other temporary jobs
- On-campus recruiting
- Résumé writing and referrals

The Career Services Office Does

- Offer advice on finding the career that is right for you,
- Give techniques for interviewing effectively, and
- Present employment opportunities.

The Career Services Office Does Not

- Tell you what career you should go for,
- Go on interviews for you, or
- Force you to take advantage of the employment opportunities.

Many students fail to take advantage of the services offered at the placement office. You don't have to be one of those who do. Persistence will be necessary as you work with the placement office. After all, this is your career. If you sign up for a job or an interview and you haven't heard from them, don't wait. Call them.

It's Off to Work We Go

The following sections describe job avenues you can discover, either through the placement office or on your own.

CAMPUS JOBS

You can gain work experience in your chosen field on or off campus. If you have time to spare, why not spend it gaining valuable work experience? If you're still a student, find a job that suits your class schedule—school is your first priority. The placement office at your college has job listings. Don't forget to check out the notice boards around campus.

If you can't find a job in your chosen field but would still like to work, find a job that suits your interests or offers an opportunity to learn new skills. Work experience is always valuable, even if it does not fall in your chosen field.

If you've recently graduated and would like to stay in academia, your college might be the ideal place of employment. After all, you're well acquainted with life on campus. Many former students wind up working at their alma maters or a related school. One graduate of the University of Illinois (Urbana/Champaign) wound up working as an admissions counselor at the University of Illinois (Chicago Campus). Check with the placement office or a specific department for job requirements.

INTERNSHIPS

Internships offer you a taste of the workplace—a chance to work in your chosen field. Both you and the company benefit. You gain valuable work experience, while they gain a willing worker. Some internships are paid positions; some offer work experience with no pay. While working for no pay may seem unfair, it might have long-term advantages. For instance, an internship could lead to a full-time position within the company.

Some fields of study require internship experience from a student or a recent graduate. Want to work in radio? An internship at a radio station could help. Want to write for a newspaper or work in publishing? An internship helps.

Let's face it—some internships are glorified "gofer" positions. Yet they do provide exposure to the daily workings of a business or ministry.

Internships through the Internet. Check these sites for internships:

www.4work.com

www.jobtrak.com

www.tripod.com

www.jobsource.com

Use these search engines for other internship avenues:

www.altavista.digital.com

www.yahoo.com

www.switchboard.com

www.hotbot.com

www.lycos.com

www.infoseek.com

www.excite.com

OTHER AVENUES FOR JOBS

Pounding the pavement may take you in these directions:

Classified ads. There are job listings in the newspaper *every day*. Sundays offer more listings.

Employment agencies. You'll find listings of these private agencies in the phone book. When you register with an employment agency, a counselor helps you with your job search. Employment agencies receive fees from employers who hire their clients. Some agencies charge their fees to the clients. If you find an agency that demands a fee from you, try to find another one.

Government agencies. Government-run employment agencies will not charge a fee to find a job for you. Have your résumé and reference list on hand. Be prepared to wait!

Temporary agencies. Some agencies specialize in temporary work. The agency sends you to different companies requesting temporary employees. You receive a paycheck from the agency. Working temporarily for a company could help you gain a full-time job within that company.

WWW.Work. There are many job-search databases on the Web, including:

www.4work.com

www.jobtrak.com

www.jobsource.com

EAGER TO INTERVIEW

Everyone job hunting has to expect an interview of some kind.

You've already had one interview at least when you first applied at your college. (If you worked through the summers, you've had others.) The job interview is the process by which you and the employer learn whether you'll fit the position offered.

Before an interview, try to learn something about the company. Complete ignorance of a company does not go over well. Wear appropriate business attire to the interview. Once you're dressed for success, make sure you're not late for your appointment. Lateness already sets up a major strike against you that you may never recover from in the eyes of the interviewer. Speaking of him or her, when you meet with the interviewer, shake his or her hand firmly. Try to be as polite and enthusiastic as you can during the interview. Even though you may be nervous, you don't have to appear that way. (Silent prayer is a big help.)

After the interview, send a thank-you letter. If you haven't heard from the employer, follow up with a call after a week or so.

Remember that the process of finding a job isn't easy. It *will* take perseverance. As Jesus once said of the church in Ephesus, "I know your deeds, your hard work and your perseverance" (Revelation 2:2). Does that describe you as well?

WOW!

Resources

There are many books on the subject of job hunting. Most of these can be found in the library. A continually popular guide for job hunters is *What Color Is Your Parachute?* by Richard Nelson Bolles (Berkeley, Calif.: Ten Speed Press [get the current edition]). The book has résumé advice and other helpful hints. Your local library should have a copy.

Another book to find in your library is *The Yale Daily New Guide to Internships* by several Yale University students (New York: Kaplan Books [get the current year's edition]). The guide lists thousands of internships (arranged by majors) offered by companies across the country.

Still another helpful book is *From College to Career: Winning Résumés for College Graduates* (2d ed.) by Nancy Shuman and Adele Lewis (Hauppage, New York: Barron's Educational Series, Inc., 1993). Check your college library or bookstore.

For some jobs, it's "who you know" that counts. The people you know can be good resources in your job search. This is networking in a nutshell. If your mom works with a coworker whose sister's uncle just happens to work in the field you want to work in, you might have an "in."

To Grad School and Beyond

CHOOSING A GRAD SCHOOL

When you looked for an undergraduate school, you were just exploring your career and life options. With graduate or professional school, you've narrowed your focus. The key is to find a school that will adequately prepare you for your future profession.

Back in Moses' day, God chose skilled craftsmen to work on the Tent of Meeting and the ark of the Testimony. (See Exodus 31:1–11.) He made sure they were thoroughly equipped for what they had to do. If a graduate or professional school is where you and God have decided that you need to go, your future education is part of your equipping process.

Consider also these questions:

• What tests will I need to take?

• What employment options will be open to me as a result of this program?

• *If the field you are going into is a highly competitive one:* What is the likelihood of my being accepted into this degree program?

• *If the field you are going into is a popular one:* Will a connection to this school help me obtain a position, even if the market is already saturated with people bearing this degree? (Especially consider this if you plan to go to law school.)

• How many faculty members are there?

• How available are the faculty members?

• How many students actually complete the degree programs?

• Can I obtain fellowship money for this program?

• What percentage of its own undergraduates does this school accept?

The *Directory of Graduate Programs* (published in four volumes by Educational Testing Service) lists important facts about grad schools to help you in your search. Once you narrow your choices down to about four or five, consider a campus visit. A visit can help you narrow your choices even further.

MORE ABOUT MEDICAL SCHOOL

What do the numbers 42,000 and 16,000 have in common? Medical school slots. About 42,000 people apply for medical school, but there are only about 16,000 openings. Medical school is tough to get into—but not impossible if you have a good GPA and great MCAT scores. (See "Admissions Tests" on page 182.)

As you research med schools, you'll see the term *allopathic medicine*. "What's that?" you say. Allopathic medicine specializes in the basic sciences during the first two years of medical school. You would receive an M.D. degree, rather than D.O. (Doctor of Osteopathy). Allopathic medicine has a more universal appeal.

THE BEST BUSINESS SCHOOLS

Every year, magazines such as *Business Week*, *Money*, and *Newsweek* devote whole issues to the best business schools. Check your local library for those issues.

WHEN TO APPLY

Many people start the process of choosing a graduate or professional school a year to a year and a half before they graduate. That way, they can obtain the recommendations needed for the application process and take any necessary tests. Medical school applicants desiring early notification apply by August the year before graduation. This means the process of choosing a medical school would've begun in the sophomore year. Law school hopefuls also begin the search and application process early.

For graduate school programs, January through March (the year you graduate) are the deadline months for applications in schools with rounds admissions. This means that the school has cycles for looking at applications. Applications are reviewed by the cycle in which they are received. You might also apply in late spring and summer of graduation year if rolling admission is allowed at your school of choice. What's rolling admission? This means applications are reviewed as they are received. When the admissions slots are full, the school stops considering applications. Check the application deadlines of each college you're considering.

Medical, dental, osteopathy, podiatry, or law school students must apply through a national application program. For example, medical school students apply through the American Medical College Application Service (AMCAS). Check the admissions office for the service you need.

When you apply to grad school, you will have to fill out an application (of course) and write a personal essay. You will also need to include your transcripts, letters of recommendation, and financial aid forms. Your test scores (see "Admissions Tests") will be sent to the school. Don't forget the application fee!

PAYING FOR GRAD SCHOOL

Loans

Remember the Free Application for Federal Student Aid (FAFSA) you filled out for your undergraduate school? You'll need an FAFSA, plus a Financial Aid PROFILE, to apply for federal loans, like Stafford Loans (subsidized or unsubsidized) or Perkins Loans, for grad school too. (Law students can also apply for a Law Access Loan.) Once again, the Federal methodology is used to assess your family contribution. Loan applications can be filed over the Internet, using the FAFSA Express service. If you have a PC (with Windows), you can load this form via the Department of Education web site (www.ed.gov/offices/OPE/Students/apply/fexpress.html). You can call 1-800-801-0576 to get the form on disk. Better file early (after January 1)! When you do file, you'll receive a Student Aid Report (SAR) in the mail. For more information, write to or call the Federal Student Aid Information Center, P. O. Box 84, Washington, D.C. 20044 (1-319-337-5665).

You can borrow up to $18,500 each year. (There is a limit of $8,500 for subsidized Stafford Loans.) When you reapply each year, you'll need a Renewal FAFSA.

For more information on government loans, read the Student Guide at the Department of Education site: (www.ed.gov/prog_info/SFA/Student Guide.)

Work and Learn

There are other sources of aid available to help you pay for your degree. You could apply for a teaching assistantship. For this you receive money in exchange for teaching duties. (Remember those TAs you had? You'll become one of them!) Other avenues include filing for a research assistantship, where you are assigned research duties by your advisor, or applying for a research grant. For a grant of this type, you have to write a proposal explaining the nature of your research, how you're uniquely qualified to perform it, and how you plan to measure your research results.

Find a Fellowship

This brings up another source: the fellowship. A fel-

Helpful Bible Verses for Making Your Decision

WIDE ANGLE

"Your word is a lamp to my feet and a light for my path." (Psalm 119:105)

"All Scripture is God-breathed and is useful for teaching, rebuking, correcting and training in righteousness, so that the man of God may be thoroughly equipped for every good work." (2 Timothy 3:16–17)

"Where there is no vision, the people perish." (Proverbs 29:18 KJV)

"Hold on to instruction, do not let it go; guard it well, for it is your life." (Proverbs 4:13)

lowship is a grant with no duties attached. Some fellowships are departmental: You have to go through your degree program to apply. Some are given by specific foundations. For example, if you're planning to study math, science, or engineering, these foundations offer grants: Fannie and John Hertz Foundation Fellowship; National Defense Science and Engineering Fellowship (NDSEG); Howard Hughes Doctoral Fellowship; NASA Graduate Student Research Program (NASA GSRP) Fellowship. Minority students can apply for GEM Minorities Fellowships; Ford Foundation Minority Doctoral Fellowships; National Physical Science Consortium (NPSC) Fellowships; and NSF Minority Graduate Fellowships. Check out www.finaid.org/finaid/focus/grad.html for other fellowship programs and web.fie.com/web/mol/molinfo.htm for minority fellowship programs. Also, head to your library to research as many fellowship opportunities as you can.

In order to apply for a fellowship, you'll need letters of recommendation. You'll also need to write a proposal. This is a statement of purpose for your graduate education. What do you plan to do with your studies? How has your experience shaped your eligibility? Your proposal will then be reviewed, along with your application. Make sure you're not late submitting your application. It will not be reviewed if it is late.

Fellowships and research grants, especially the popular ones, can be tough to get. There is competition for the money. Yet it is worth the time to look into getting one. For more information on-line on financial aid for graduate students, look for www.mkant@finaid.org

ADMISSIONS TESTS

There is a test for every type of graduate or professional school. For medical schools the MCAT is a must. Law schools look at the LSAT. Business schools bank on the GMAT. Other graduate programs go for the GRE. Which test is right for you? Look below. If you need preparation, check out a Kaplan or Princeton Review course.

MCAT: MAKING THE GRADE

What is the MCAT? In a word (or four), it is the Medical College Admissions Test, written by the American Association of Medical Colleges (AAMC). The test is offered twice a year: April and August. You must register by March for the April test and July for the August test. Medical school admissions boards look at your scores as part of the admissions process. Although a basic knowledge of biology, organic chemistry, and physics is important, the test is geared to showcase how well you think. The test helps you apply your analytical-reasoning, abstract-thinking, and problem-solving skills to given situations.

LSAT: LOOKING TO THE LAW

The Law School Admissions Test (LSAT) is the test to take for—you guessed it—getting into law school. The Law School Admissions Services (LSAS) oversees the test. You can take the test in February, June, October (sometimes late September), and December.

GMAT: Going to Business School

The Graduate Management Admissions Test is the one to take when applying for M.B.A. (Master of Business Administration) programs. In days past, the test was offered in a paper-and-pencil form. That has gone the way of the dodo, as of 1997. You'll have to take the CAT (Computer Adaptive Test).

GRE: Geared Up for Grad School

The Graduate Record Exam is the exam for other graduate school programs. The GRE is offered as a paper-and-pencil test and a CAT test.

Resources

Your college's library should have plenty of material you can use to research graduate schools, including:

- *Peterson's Graduate Education Directory* (Princeton, Peterson's Guides)
- *Peterson's Grants for Graduate Students* (Princeton, Peterson's Guides)
- *Peterson's Register of Higher Education* (Princeton, Peterson's Guides)
- *Best Medical Schools* (most current edition) by Malaika Stoll and Paula Bilstein (profiles the top 139 medical schools in the country)
- *Gourman Report of Graduate Programs* (most current edition) by Jack Gourman, Ph.D. (reviews graduate and professional schools; considered to be one of the best resources for choosing a school)
- *The Official Guide to U.S. Law Schools*, by Law School Admission Council, Inc. (New York: Broadway Books)
- *Student Access Guide to the Best Medical Schools,* Princeton Review (New York: Villard Books/Random House)
- *Student Access Guide to the Best Business Schools,* Princeton Review (New York: Villard Books/Random House)

Check out these guides for test preparation:
- *Cracking the MCAT,* Princeton Review (New York: Villard Books/Random House). The Princeton Review provides techniques to help you prepare for the test and provides a sample test.
- *Kaplan GMAT* (New York: Kaplan Educational Centers and Simon & Schuster)
- *Arco Teacher Certification Tests* (New York: Macmillan). If you're planning to teach, don't forget the certification test. A book such as this will help you prepare.
- *Barron's GRE* (Hauppage, New York: Barron's Educational Series, Inc.)

Check out these sites and search engines for information on graduate and professional schools and the tests needed:
- www.gospelcom.net
- www.petersons.com
- www.gre.org (the GRE web site)
- Simon and Schuster's College On-line (Keyword: *College On-line* on AOL; has links to web sites like www.kaplan.com)
- The Princeton Review On-line (one of the Learning and Culture web sites on AOL)
- www.kaplan.com (for more information on MCAT, LSAT, GMAT, and GRE; the site has sample tests)
- www.collegenet.com
- www.collegeedge.com
- www.altavista.digital.com
- www.yahoo.com/Education
- www.csearch.kaplan.com

For financial aid information, look for these sites:
- www.ed.gov (the Department of Education's web site)
- www.finaid.org/finaid/focus/grad.html (information on financial aid for grad students)
- www.ets.org (check the "Student Loan Counselor" section of the GRE site link)
- www.act.org/financial/aid/index.html (part of the American College Testing web site)